Preparing for a Career in Travel & Hospitality

Ferguson Publishing Company, Chicago, Illinois

Printed in the United States of America
V-4

Library of Congress Cataloging-in-Publication Data

Preparing for a career in travel & hospitality.
        p.   cm. -- (What can I do now?)
    Includes bibliographical references and index.
    Summary: Introduces the travel and hospitality industries, presents informtion about careers in these fields, and suggests what to do now to prepare for future work in these areas.
    ISBN 0-89434-253-3
    1. Hospitality industry--Vocational guidance. 2. Tourist trade--Vocational guidance. [1. Hospitality industry--Vocational guidance. 2. Tourist trade--Vocational guidance. 3. Vocational guidance.] I. J.G. Ferguson Publishing Company. II. Series.
    TX911.3.V62P74   1998
    647.94'023--dc21   98-19885
                                                CIP
                                                AC

Ferguson Publishing Company
200 West Madison, Suite 300
Chicago, Illinois 60606
800-306-9941
www.fergpubco.com

About
the Staff

Holli Cosgrove, *Editorial Director*

Andrew Morkes, *Editor*

Veronica Melnyk, *Assistant Editor*

Shawna Brynildssen, Felicitas Cortez, Veronica Melnyk, Beth Oakes, Elizabeth Taggart, *Writers*

Connie Rockman, MLS; Alan Wieder, *Bibliographers*

Patricia Murray, Bonnie Needham, *Proofreaders*

Joe Grossmann, *Interior Design*

Parameter Design, *Cover Design*

Contents

Introduction

If you are considering a career in travel and hospitality—which presumably you are since you're reading this book—you must realize that the better informed you are from the start, the better your chances of having a successful, satisfying career.

There is absolutely no reason to wait until you get out of high school to "get serious" about a career. That doesn't mean you have to make a firm, undying commitment right now. Gasp! Indeed, one of the biggest fears most people face at some point (sometimes more than once) is choosing the right career. Frankly, many people don't "choose" at all. They take a job because they need one, and all of a sudden ten years have gone by and they wonder why they're stuck doing something they hate. Don't be one of those people! You have the opportunity right now-while you're still in high school and still relatively unencumbered with major adult responsibilities-to explore, to experience, to try out a work path. Or several paths if you're one of those overachieving types. Wouldn't you really rather find out sooner than later that you're not cut out to be a pilot after all, that you'd actually prefer to be a travel agent? Or a flight attendant? Or an adventure travel specialist?

There are many ways to explore the travel and hospitality industry. What we've tried to do in this book is give you an idea of some of your options. The chapter "What Do I Need to Know about Travel & Hospitality" will give you an overview of the field-a little history, where it's at today, and promises of the future; as well as a breakdown of its structure-how it's organized-and a glimpse of some of its many career options.

The Careers section includes ten chapters, each describing in detail a specific career in the travel and hospitality industry: adventure travel specialist, flight attendant, hotel concierge, hotel desk clerk, hotel executive housekeeper, hotel manager, hotel restaurant manager, pilot, tour guide, and travel agent. The educational requirements for these specialties range from high school diploma to bachelor's degree. These chapters rely heavily on first-hand accounts from real people on the job. They'll tell you what skills you need, what personal qualities you have to have, what the ups and downs of the jobs are. You'll also find out about educational requirements-including specific high school and college classes-advancement possibilities, related jobs, salary ranges, and the future outlook.

The real meat of the book is in the section called "What Can I Do Right Now?" This is where you get busy and DO SOMETHING. The chapter "Get Involved" will clue you in on the obvious-volunteering and interning-and the not-so-obvious-summer camps and summer college study, high school hospitality programs, and student organizations.

In keeping with the secondary theme of this book (the primary theme, for those of you who still don't get it, is "You can do something now"), the chapter "Do It Yourself" urges you to take charge and start your own programs and activities where none exist-school, community, or even national. Why not?

While we think the best way to explore travel and hospitality is to jump right in and start doing it, there are plenty of other ways to get into the industry's mind-set. "Surf the Web" offers you a short annotated list of travel and hospitality Web sites where you can explore everything from job listings (start getting an idea of what employers are looking for now) to educational and certification requirements to on-the-job accounts.

"Read a Book" is an annotated bibliography of books (some new, some old) and periodicals. If you're even remotely considering a career in travel and hospitality, reading a few books and checking out a few magazines is the easiest thing you can do. Don't stop with our list. Ask your librarian to point you to more materials. Keep reading!

"Ask for Money" is a sampling of travel and hospitality scholarships. You need to be familiar with these because you're going to need money for school. You have to actively pursue scholarships; no one is going to come up to you in the hall one day and present you with a check because you're such a wonderful student. Applying for scholarships is work. It takes effort. And it must be done right and often a year in advance of when you need the money.

"Look to the Pros" is the final chapter. It's a list of professional organizations that you can turn to for more information about accredited schools, education requirements, career descriptions, salary information, job listings, scholarships, and much more. Once you become a nursing student, you'll be able to join many of these. Time after time, professionals say that membership and active participation in a professional organization is one of the best ways to network (make valuable contacts) and gain recognition in your field.

High school can be a lot of fun. There are dances and football games; maybe you're in band or play a sport. Great! Maybe you hate school and are just biding your time until you graduate. Too bad. Whoever you are take a minute and try to imagine your life five years from now. Ten years from now. Where will you be? What will you be doing? Whether you realize it or not, how you choose to spend your time now-studying, playing, watching TV, working at a fast food restaurant, hanging out, whatever-will have an impact on your future. Take a look at how you're spending your time now and ask yourself, "Where is this getting me?" If you can't come up with an answer, it's probably "nowhere." The choice is yours. No one is going to take you by the hand and lead you in the "right" direction. It's up to you. It's your life. You can do something about it right now!

WHAT DO I
NEED TO KNOW ABOUT

Travel &
Hospitality
?

The idea of travel

is a glamorous one. When you think of travel, you may picture yourself sipping café au lait in a Parisian sidewalk café. You may imagine going on safari in Africa. Or perhaps your idea of travel is merely relaxing in a fancy five-star hotel that places foil-wrapped chocolates on your pillow. Or a more realistic one of traveling on a family vacation and spending the night at a quaint mom-and-pop operation—you know, the kind with a fenced (chain-linked, of course) in-ground pool. Maybe you'd rather relax in a deck chair on board a cruise ship—or go deep-sea diving in the Caribbean.

Whatever your travel fantasy is, however, it probably doesn't include some important details—like how you're going to get there. Or where you're going to stay. Or finding the best price on airfare and car rentals. Or how your money converts to the local currency. Even though these details may not be included in your travel fantasy, they are nonetheless essential elements of any trip. The individuals we rely on to handle those details, and to get us comfortably from point A to point B, are those who work in the travel and hospitality industry.

Not all careers in travel and hospitality require that you actually travel. There is, in fact, a very broad range of career opportunities that require no travel at all. It is perhaps easiest to look at the travel and hospitality industry as broken down into two major divisions: planning and execution. That is, there are thousands of people working just to help travelers plan their trips. These individuals check fares, book seats on airplanes, reserve rental cars and hotel rooms, and provide information on planned destinations—but they have nothing to do with the actual trip itself. These are the people working in the planning division.

Workers in the execution division actually deal with travelers while they are on their trips. They are the pilots who fly the airplanes, the flight attendants who seat and serve air travelers, and the tour guides who oversee groups of travelers. They are the concierges in hotels who give tips on hot destinations, the executive housekeepers who provide you with a clean and comfortable room, and the restaurant managers who make sure you have a good meal at the start or end of your exciting vacation or business day.

Many jobs in the execution division require you to be very mobile. Other jobs, however, such as travel agent, airline or rental car reservation agent, or hotel desk clerk, allow you the convenience of a routine one-location job. Depending upon your personal desires and needs, you can pursue a travel and hospitality job that turns you into a world traveler or one that lets you come home for dinner every night.

Many careers in the travel branch of the travel and hospitality industry rarely require a college degree; instead, they usually require specialized training. In some cases, this training is provided on the job. Most airlines, for example, have extensive training programs for their employees—from baggage handlers to flight attendants to ticket agents. In other cases, training can be obtained through independent schools or training programs. There are many such independent training programs for travel agents. And even though a degree is rarely required, there are certainly many college graduates working in the field as well as in management positions. In travel, as in most industries, the more education you have, the better your chances for advancement.

Though a degree in hotel management is increasingly preferred for upper management, accounting, marketing and sales, and other executive positions, a college education is not a requirement for most other jobs in the hospitality branch of the travel and hospitality field. Bellhops, housekeepers, switchboard operators, and desk clerks are among the many entry-level jobs available to recent high school graduates, or even students wishing to hold part-time jobs while in high school. This is an

Lingo to Learn

Airlines Reporting Corporation (ARC): *An independent corporation created by domestic airlines, which governs and regulates payments to airlines and commission fees to travel agencies.*

City codes: *Three-letter codes used to uniquely identify cities and/or their airports.*

Customs: *A government agency that monitors the flow of goods and substances into and from a country.*

Ground arrangements: *Services covering the land portion of a trip, such as lodging, transportation, sightseeing, and meals.*

Hub-and-spoke: *A system many airlines have adopted to maximize the amount of time their planes spend in the air; designating certain cities as hubs, scheduling many flights to them, and offering connecting flights from the hubs to smaller cities, which can be served by smaller aircraft.*

Itinerary: *The route of travel.*

Package: *A travel product bundling several distinct elements, such as air travel, a rental car, and a hotel.*

Passport: *A document identifying an individual as a citizen of a specific country and attesting to his or her ability to travel freely.*

Terminal: *An airport, train station, or bus station.*

Visa: *A document or, more frequently, a stamp in a passport authorizing the bearer to visit a country for specific purposes for a specific length of time.*

industry that truly rewards experience. It is not uncommon to hear of former busboys or bellhops rising to the rank of banquet manager or general manager. To accomplish this purpose, hotels and motels run an intricate system of keeping house. There is a job for every talent and interest within the growing hotel and motel industry. If you are skillful in organizing and helping people, maybe a job as a desk or reservation clerk is for you. Do you feel most at ease when planning a dinner or party? If so, then a position in the banquet department sounds just right. Are you "in the know" when it comes to the best restaurant or hottest ticket in town? Then you should find out what other interests and skills it takes to become a concierge. Most important, whatever department grabs your attention, remember that the lodging trade is all about serving the guest. Candidates with a pleasant personality and desire to help will succeed. No hotheads need apply!

Whatever your talent, whatever your level of education, read on and learn if a career in travel and hospitality is for you. This book will try to give you a broad overview of the many career options available to you in travel and hospitality—and how you can start preparing for them right now.

GENERAL INFORMATION

Hotels and motels have always existed in some form or another as long as people have needed to travel long distances, requiring an overnight stay. These structures were built along trading routes followed by travelers long before the first roads were built. The earliest lodging places, called *inns*, most likely offered little more than a sheltered area, usually by a source of water. In many parts of the world, it was the custom for people to offer a resting place to weary travelers in their homes.

When the Roman Empire was at the peak of its power in AD 100, it built the first great system of roads. These cobblestone roads were the most extensive, well-constructed roads ever seen, covering more than fifty thousand miles. While this road system was constructed by and for the Roman troops, it was used mainly by people in commerce and trade to transport goods between Rome and other cities. Eventually, inns and restaurants developed along the roads to accommodate the needs of travelers on long journeys. As transportation improved, the number of people traveling increased. Pilgrimages to the holy lands, sacred places, and the sites of miracles became common undertakings for the population. Long voyages of several hundred and several thousand miles were made by those in search of adventure or commerce. Eventually, travel began to be accepted for the sake of entertainment and enjoyment. It provided a diversion for those with sufficient time and money.

In America, the first public inn was built in Jamestown, Virginia, in 1607. Most of the early American hotels were established on the East Coast, where travelers from Europe would disembark. Inns, taverns, and *ordinaries,* as they were called in the southern colonies, appeared along canals, rivers, seaports, and roads. As the country expanded into the western territories, farmhouse inns were maintained along the stagecoach routes.

Technology began to make travel much easier and more affordable in the nineteenth century. Starting in the late eighteenth and early nineteenth centuries, inventors competed to develop the first steam-powered locomotives. By the 1830s, the first workable engines and rail lines carried goods and passengers throughout the Atlantic states. In 1852, the first train reached Chicago, and soon the new towns in the Mississippi Valley had railway service to the Eastern seaports. The West and East were finally linked by a rail line in 1869, when the First Continental Railway was completed. The rise of the railroads increased the demand for hotels and inns in both Europe and the United States. Having a railroad stop was usually a boon to small towns. Hotels were usually located close to the train station; they also grew larger to accommodate the increasing numbers of travelers.

Starting in the second half of the nineteenth century, steamships gradually replaced sailing vessels on the world's trade and passenger routes. Passenger travel between Europe and the States increased. Luxury cruise ships—to carry passengers to and from Europe—were built with the best accommodations that could be put on a ship. These vessels featured orchestras, ballrooms, fine dining halls, and such. The *Queen Elizabeth* was probably one of the best known, most traveled of the luxury liners. Ship travel was intended to be leisurely. Crossing the Atlantic by ship took two weeks.

With the new methods of travel, tourism was no longer limited to the "idle rich." The working class could afford train fare to the countryside or the big cities. For Americans, a trip to Europe became an achievable goal; although the cost was still quite high, it was within the grasp of enough people to save for and plan the trip. In the late nineteenth and early twentieth centuries, a trip abroad was a regular gift to the graduating college student. Referred to commonly as a "grand tour," it was seen as a reward as well as a learning experience for the college graduate.

A new age of travel began when the Wright brothers made the first successful powered flight of a heavier-than-air craft in 1903. Within a few decades,

Monasteries: Our Early Hotels

In addition to our earliest inns, travelers could also find lodging at monasteries; eventually monasteries developed separate dormitory lodgings for such visitors, and it was the regular responsibility of some of the monks to tend to the guests' needs. The Le Grand Saint Bernard Hospice in the Swiss Alps—featuring the famous St. Bernard dogs—was founded in AD 961 by Augustinian monks specifically as an inn for travelers. This huge stone structure was one of the earliest identified inns and had up to 80 beds with the capacity of sheltering a total of 300 persons.

the airplane had secured its place as a vital means of transportation. As the airline industry developed, advancements in plane design allowed for a greater number of passengers on a greater number of routes. Small cities were able to establish airports for smaller vehicles, and large cities found themselves with several runways and substantial air traffic.

As the number of travelers increased, hotel and motel owners began to compete for customers by creating more luxurious and service-oriented establishments. Lodgings began to offer more than a bed, a meal, and a roof over one's head. People began to have parties and meetings at inns. The size of the average hotel increased. The largest hotels would have hundreds of rooms. During the nineteenth century, many luxury hotels were established to cater to the well-to-do traveler. These hotels featured dining rooms, ballrooms, shops, billiard and sitting rooms, and other amenities, in addition to many clean, well-appointed rooms. Often as large and as opulent as palaces, these hotels *de grand luxe* appeared in the major cities of the United States and Europe. The Ritz hotels of London, New York, and Paris, the Palace Hotel of San Francisco, and the Waldorf Astoria of New York were famous for their luxurious accommodations.

Due to the growing interest in and popularity of commercial travel, the need for people who could plan trips increased. Travel agents who knew which hotels were good, how to get reservations, and how to make travel plans found themselves increasingly in demand. Thomas Cook, in England, began his business with the guided tour in 1841. He specialized in excursions that serviced hundreds of thousands of people a year. Exotic places like Egypt and the Orient were open to travelers on the Cook tours. Travel agencies developed everywhere in the West. Travel specialists who could arrange tours and travel guides who knew the ins and outs of faraway places became sought-after businesspeople. The booming travel industry relied on experts to steer tourists to their establishments.

Until the twentieth century, travelers had little to choose between the luxury hotels on the one end and the inexpensive hotels, which were not always very clean or comfortable, on the other. This changed when Ellsworth Statler (1863-1928) began building his chain of mid-priced Statler Hotels, which set a new standard for the quality, amenities, and service the middle-class traveler could expect. Statler's hotels featured clean, comfortable rooms, each with a private bath, telephone, radio, full-length mirror, and closet, for a modest price. Coordinating linens, china, and silverware were used in each Statler hotel restaurant, as well as standardized recipes.

Freestanding (or self-contained) restaurants once were associated almost exclusively with hotels. Prohibition and the 1920s dramatically altered that association. Before the Volstead Act, which outlawed the consumption of alcohol in the United States, hotel guests could relax with a drink in the downstairs bar or restaurant. Denied their drinks during Prohibition, they left their hotels in the evening to scout the neighborhood for one of the many speakeasies that served liquor illegally. Most of the speakeasies also provided food, both to cover their illegal activities and to please their customers. Thus, Prohibition helped drive a wedge between the hotel and the restaurant, two institutions that traditionally had coexisted for mutual profit.

More dramatic changes for the hotel profession came with the rise of the automobile. A new type of hotel appeared to cater to the increasing mobility of the public. Motor inns and travel courts, often built by farmers where their land faced onto one of the new roads being built all across the country to meet the needs of the motoring population, offered far simpler accommodations than a hotel. Despite an early reputation as a gathering place for thieves and other undesirable people, motor inns—later called motels (a contraction of the words motor and hotel), soon drew off much of the business from the city-based hotels. Motels gained an image as inexpensive, simple lodging places offering convenient automobile parking for guests. However, modern motels have become larger, fancier establishments with conference and ballroom facilities, as well other amenities comparable to larger hotels, so the quality distinctions between the two are almost nonexistent.

The hotels responded to this new competition by building or expanding their facilities to accommodate large meetings and conventions. More and more self-standing restaurants appeared, many offering simple, quick fare to motorists. The automobile made even the most remote locations accessible, and resorts were built to cater to every type of vacationer.

The biggest boom in the hotel and motel industry came with the end of World War II. More and more people were purchasing cars, and with a healthy economy and growing amounts of leisure time, more people were traveling, dining out, and vacationing than ever before. Hotel chains such as the Statler and Hilton hotels were soon joined by chains of motels, such as Howard Johnson and Holiday Inn. Entire cities became devoted to the hotel industry,

Fast Fact

such as the gambling city of Las Vegas, or seaside resort towns such as Atlantic City. The growth of the airline industry in the 1950s made long-distance travel still more practical, and created a demand for new hotels, now located near the airports.

One trend in the hotel and motel industry of the last several decades has been toward consolidation. Today, over 50 percent of the hotel and motel beds in the United States are controlled by about 25 companies. The world's largest lodging system is Holiday Inns, Inc., with 359,000 guest rooms throughout its 2,200 properties; Best Western follows with 3,463 properties totaling 281,700 guest rooms.

A second trend in the hospitality industry is the growing popularity of bed and breakfasts (B & Bs), which offer a personal touch to the tourist or business person tired of staying in impersonal chain hotels and motels. Bed and breakfasts offer overnight lodging to guests in a distinctive way. B & Bs are usually private homes, farmhouses, or other historic or period buildings with a small number of rooms. The most successful B & Bs are pleasant and homey creations, where the friendly touch of the owners make each visit a personal and memorable experience for travelers. There are thousands of bed and breakfasts in the United States.

A third trend in the hospitality industry has been the construction of increasing numbers of retirement communities; as people live longer, and retire with more wealth, these self-contained communities offer private homes clustered around meeting, recreation, and dining facilities.

In the past, hotels and motels were set up primarily to serve the wealthy traveler or the person going from place to place. Today, with places such as Disney World, Universal Studios, Club Med, and others, many hotels are no longer simply places to stay while visiting a certain location. They have become travel destinations in themselves.

STRUCTURE OF THE INDUSTRY

There are four basic necessities of travel. These are transportation, lodging, dining, and entertainment. When planning a trip, most travelers first gather information on these four elements by checking the current availability and cost of transportation, lodging, and food at their planned destination. The entertainment aspects of the destination are considered as well. Some locations are interesting for their historical or cultural relevance, others provide pleasant natural surroundings, while yet others provide physical adventure. The tourist may choose to combine one or more elements in a package plan that someone else arranges, or the tourist may choose to create a vacation and handle all the planning personally. In both instances, travel specialists may be involved in providing guidance, information, and services to the traveler.

If the traveler is planning a trip without the aid of a travel specialist, or travel agent, the resources available are varied, depending on the destination. A number of written travel guides are available for almost every major destination, whether it's a city or a natural area, and travel guides for entire regions and countries are also abundant. Language books for travel abroad give translations and pronunciation guides for commonly used phrases. Cassette tapes are also available for travelers who wish to learn a little of the local language before heading abroad. Classes, television shows, and an endless variety of compact discs, cassettes, and books are available for foreign language instruction specifically geared to the traveler. All the commonly studied languages are widely available and many of the more unfamiliar languages, such as African tribal languages, are also available.

Many travelers find it easier to let a professional help them with the information gathering and planning. In this case, they consult a *travel agency*. The goal of travel agents working for a travel agency is to help their clients plan a trip that meets their desires and fits within their travel budget. Specifically, they check rates on transportation and accommodations and for make transportation and hotel reservations. Agents also provide information such as visa and medical requirements for travel abroad, and they supply additional directions specific to the traveler's need.

There is another option for travelers that simplifies the planning process even more: the packaged tour. Packaged tours—which can range from several days to several weeks—are available for those who wish to have many aspects of a trip planned in advance. They may cover a number of countries or they may stay in one city the entire time. Tourists have a wide variety of tours to choose from to meet their specific needs and interests. Travel agencies, private groups, museums, universities, and other institutions are just some of the organizations that provide package tours.

One specific type of packaged tour is adventure travel, which has become one of the fastest growing segments of the travel industry. This type of travel is geared toward the more physically active traveler who enjoys both seeing great wonders and scaling or exploring them, too. Adrenaline-pumping activities such as kayaking, whitewater rafting, and hiking are just some of the

Fast Fact

As of 1995, the U.S. government had allocated $16 million annually for tourism promotion. This ranked the United States thirty-third in terms of national government tourism promotion budgets—well behind such countries as Greece and Spain, both of which spent well in excess of $100 million.

pursuits available to the adventure traveler. Hundreds of outfitters make a living organizing and guiding such trips, which may include a week-long trip sea-kayaking in Baja or white-water rafting in the Grand Canyon. Outfitters usually specialize in one sport, but some of the bigger companies take on more than one. They usually take groups of eight or more people on their trips.

For tourists interested in spending much of the time actually moving from one point to another, cruise ships provide a slower, more leisurely type of travel. Cruise ships were the only form of travel across the oceans for many years. With the onset of air travel, cruise ships fell out of favor. Shorter cruises, in the Caribbean, for example, have once again gained in popularity. Cruise ships provide enough entertainment so that some passengers regard them as floating vacation spas. The locations visited by the ship may not be that important to the cruise passengers who choose whether or not to disembark at ports. Cruises usually run from three days to a few weeks and may dock in two or three cities. Some of the most popular cruises of the 1990s were to the Arctic, the Antarctic, and Alaska. The rugged terrain and remote wilderness provide an ideal view from the water.

Establishments in the hotel and motel industry fall into one of five categories: transient, motel or motor inns, residential, resort, and convention hotels.

Transient, also known as commercial, hotels make up three-fourths of the hotel business in the United States. These hotels cater to commercial travelers, businesspeople, salespeople, and tourists who wish to spend one or more nights at the hotel. Many commercial hotels have swimming pools, saunas, exercise rooms, ballrooms, conference rooms, and some house restaurants and drinking establishments open to the public as well as guests.

Motels are generally located near highways and airports and in small cities. Many motels offer parking beside or near the guest's room, eliminating any garage fees and unnecessary nightly loading and unloading of baggage. The facilities range from simply a room with a bathroom to motels with swimming pools and restaurants. Others have rooms that are designed as separate structures, each with a bed, bathroom, and kitchenette. These accommodations are referred to as suites. Some hotels offer suites only, mainly housing businesspeople on extended stays.

An inn is usually a small building, perhaps an extension of somebody's home, that provides simple services such as a clean bed and bathroom. The number of rooms range from five to twenty. A growing branch of inns have become bed and breakfasts.

Residential hotels provide permanent or semipermanent housing, on a weekly, monthly, or sometimes yearly, payment basis. These facilities may offer amenities such as maid and food service. Some residential hotels may provide small kitchenettes in each room.

Hotels that offer recreational or social activities besides lodgings are considered resorts. Usually located near popular tourist attractions, resorts may have skiing, or during warmer weather, water activities, tennis, golf, or horseback riding, among others, to keep guests busy. Many of these hotels offer fine shopping and dining, themed decor and entertainment. The resort as a complete family vacation destination is an apparent trend. Hawaii, Florida, Mexico, and the Caribbean are meccas of luxury resorts. Some resorts, especially those in Las Vegas and Atlantic City, are built around gambling activities.

Spas are similar to resorts, but differ in that usually everything required for the vacation is present in one location. If the guest decides he or she does not want to leave the grounds until the end of the vacation, the facilities provide everything from food to entertainment to keep the guests happy. The spas may choose to have an operating theme, such as physical health care, and many of the day's activities will focus on that. A health spa will include health-conscious menus, exercise classes, massages, relaxation therapy, and other aspects of health training and support.

Convention centers are usually a complex of buildings, one of which is a hotel. These centers are used as meeting places for large groups or business-es, or for major exhibitions; lodgings for the conventioneers are provided by the adjoining hotel. Convention hotels and centers must have state-of-the-art audiovisual and technical equipment to stay competitive. Many of these convention centers are found in desirable, tourist-friendly locations, such as Las Vegas.

There are seven main branches of the hotel and motel industry. Front office, service, marketing and sales, and accounting comprise the "front of the house" positions, or those most visible to the public. Less visible "back of the house" jobs include food and beverage, housekeeping, and engineering and maintenance. Most branches of this industry operate on a three-shift system, allowing for twenty-four-hour service for hotel guests.

The front office deals with all the paper and computer work involved with room and reservation assignments. The people working in this department also run the reservation desk, switchboard, and mail room. A general manager heads this department as well as the entire hotel operation and employees. Department supervisors report to the general manager.

The main purpose of the service branch is to make the guests feel welcome. This includes greeting guests, parking cars, running the elevators, opening doors, carrying baggage, preparing a guest's room, and assisting with travel plans and entertainment. Most jobs in this department need little training or further education, thus creating a great starting place for employees eager to break into the hotel trade.

Fast Fact

More than 30,000 travel agencies operate in the United States and Canada.

The accounting and financial management branch controls the fiscal affairs of the hotel. Projects such as financial policy and planning, maintenance of records and statements, overseeing expenditures, bank accounts, and payroll handling are some of the many responsibilities of this department. Though the accounting staff may not have one-on-one contact with hotel guests, this department is considered "front of the house" because the nature of the work is managerial. Many of the accounting executives rise to leading hotel positions.

The marketing and sales sector strives to attract potential customers. The employees of this department try to find out what guests need and desire to make their establishment more appealing. Marketing and sales workers often use surveys, focus groups, or other research methods to gauge the feelings and opinions of guests and potential guests. The creative efforts of those in marketing and sales are expressed in new programs to attract guests or promotional campaigns designed to inform potential guests of current services.

The food and beverage departments are among the largest and most lucrative sectors in the hospitality industry. It includes all the services involved with the bars and restaurants of a hotel, as well as room service, from purchasing, and food preparation to presentation.

Depending on the size of the hotel, the housekeeping department can easily number in the hundreds. The room and floor attendants are responsible for keeping the rooms clean and supplied with fresh linens and towels. They also suggest repairs and improvements for guest rooms.

The engineering and maintenance departments keep the facilities of a hotel, motel, or similar establishment in working order. The chores include plumbing, painting, electrical wiring, and general repairing. They also help the housekeeping staff with the heavier tasks of keeping a hotel clean.

CAREERS

We can break down the wide variety of careers available in the travel and hospitality industry by again keeping in mind the four basic necessities of travel—transportation, lodging, dining, and entertainment. A sampling of career opportunities in each area follows. The ultimate goal is the same for everyone in the industry: customer service and satisfaction.

TRANSPORTATION (TRIP PLANNING)

Before the fun or business of a trip can begin, it must be planned; travel and lodging reservations must be made, rental cars reserved, entertainment possibilities explored. A variety of workers help people plan and organize their travel itineraries.

Reservation agents, for example, may work for hotels, airlines, health spas, train lines, cruise ships, or a number of other facilities directly related to one form of trip or another. They are responsible for checking the availability of accommodations and reserving a place for the customer. Agents confirm schedules, arrival times, departure times, and all the necessary information to ensure smooth travel arrangements. Some agents can issue tickets, depending upon the tour companies they work for.

Like a reservation agent, the *ticket agent* is responsible for finding an open place for a customer, usually on a plane, and verifying the schedule of arrival, departure, and other necessary information. *Car rental agents* fill requests from travelers who require a vehicle while in the area.

For clients seeking specific assistance and information on certain types of travel, a *travel consultant* is available to help customize a vacation or travel plan. This assistance may include obtaining a visa for foreign travel, arranging special accommodations for the client, or adapting a schedule to fit the client's needs.

Serving some of the same functions as the travel consultant, the *travel agent* also issues tickets and reservations and may be able to design group packages and tours for a number of clients traveling together. Travel agents may specialize in one region or one form of transportation. They make their income from commissions paid by the airlines and the destinations to which they book their clients.

Travelers traveling by plane are taken care of during the flight by *flight attendants.* These workers, who spend most of their working hours in the air, help passengers board the plane, stow their luggage, and find seats. They also serve drinks and food during the trip, try to meet any specific needs a traveler may have, and ensure that passengers follow airline safely regulations.

Commercial airline pilots are those who actually fly the planes that carry passengers. They are responsible for rigidly following flight plans that dictate route, speed, and departure and arrival times. While en route, they monitor aircraft systems, watch weather conditions, and maintain constant communication with the air traffic controller. There are three main designations of commercial airline pilots: *captain, copilot,* and *flight engineer.*

Vacation tour guides sometimes accompany travelers on their trips. They provide assistance with accommodations, foreign languages, logistics of travel, and information about the places that will be visited while traveling. The tour guide is often responsible for arranging everything from transportation to and from airports to the menu to be served in the restaurants where the tour members will eat. In many locations, such as castles, museums, and historical sites, group tour guides present the place in an educated manner with information that the tourist may not know.

Adventure travel outfitters plan and lead trips for physically active or sports-minded groups of people to exotic places both here and abroad. The successful outfitter will have a great deal of travel experience in the area in which he or she specializes. He or she usually has an office staff and a field staff of guides who actually lead the trips.

LODGING

Chances are you have stayed at one of over forty-four thousand hotels and motels found throughout the United States. These places, from the grand luxury of the Waldorf Astoria, to the Bates Motel, to the more ubiquitous HoJo, may differ in levels of accommodations (not to mention room service, or lack thereof); but all do share the same basic purpose of providing safe and comfortable lodging for travelers.

When people travel away from home they obviously need a comfortable place to stay and relax. All hotel and motel centers need conscientious, well-trained employees. Since customer contact is a rudimentary element of any hotel industry position, it is helpful for employees to possess good communication skills, patience, a diplomatic demeanor, and a readiness to help.

By dividing the work of a hotel into *front-of-the-house,* where employees are highly visible to the guests, and *back-of-the-house,* where employees generally work behind the scenes, we can get a better understanding of the various opportunities available in the hotel and motel industry.

Front-of-the-House

Doorkeepers and baggage porters, also known as *bellhops,* help guests as they arrive at or depart from the hotel. They often direct customers to the check-in counter and then usher them to their rooms. Bellhops sometimes assist guests in hailing taxis. *Bell captains* supervise bellhops and doorkeepers.

Administrative positions, such as *desk and reservation clerks,* account for 15 percent of jobs in the lodging industry. Their many duties include coordinating reservations and room assignments, greeting guests, furnishing room keys or key cards, and forwarding mail and any messages. Front office workers also handle complaints and are often the employees guests turn to most frequently for assistance.

The position of the *concierge* started as a European custom, but now is a staple in many larger urban hotels. Among their many duties, the concierge can handle requests for special services such as reserving theater or sports tickets. Since a concierge may be asked for recommendations to restaurants, museums, or other entertainment options, he or she must be well versed in the city's cultural and tourist attractions. Most concierges are multilingual to better serve international guests.

Each area of the hotel—from the restaurant to security to the front desk—requires managers. *Restaurant managers* oversee the daily operations of the hotel's restaurant or restaurants. They report to the food and beverage manager, who is responsible for all food and beverage services in the hotel. (See the "Dining" section below for more information on these types of managers.) A *security manager,* sometimes known as a *director of hotel security,* is entrusted with the protection of the guests, workers, and grounds and property of the hotel. *Resident managers* live in the hotel and are on-call twenty-four hours a day in case an emergency or other situation requires immediate action. They supervise all the hotel departments, as well as handle guest complaints. *Front office managers* supervise all front office personnel and activities, including scheduling work assignments for these workers, creating and managing reservations systems, and overseeing guest relations. *General managers* supervise the overall operations of a hotel establishment. They coordinate front desk service, bell service, housekeeping, and other aspects of day-to-day operations.

The financial department oversees all money that comes into a hotel. It is responsible for recording sales, controlling expenditures, and keeping track of overall profits or losses. Financial employees include *controllers, head accountants, cost accountants, credit managers, accounts receivable supervisors, accounts payable supervisors,* and *bookkeepers.*

Sales and marketing staffs are part of the larger hotels and franchise operations. The *director of marketing and sales* oversees a staff of *sales managers* and *sales and marketing workers.* As *public relations specialists,* sales and marketing staff constantly strive to keep the hotel's identity before the public by arranging for favorable radio, television, newspaper, and magazine publicity and by seeking additional business clientele. Sales and marketing workers also often conduct surveys designed to monitor the feelings and opinions of guests or potential guests.

The human resources or personnel department is responsible for hiring and firing the employees of a hotel. They also make sure that employees are productive and happy in their duties. The *personnel manager* heads the department. Larger hotels employ *training managers,* who oversee the hotel's management training program. Other employees in this department include *benefits coordinators,* who handle employee benefits such as health insurance and pension plans, and *employee relations managers,* who deal with employee rights and grievances with an overall goal of creating a positive and productive work atmosphere.

Fast Fact

Young people ages 18 to 24 have been the traditional major source of entry-level labor in the hospitality industry.

Back-of-the-House

The housekeeping staff is responsible for keeping guestrooms and the rest of the hotel clean and orderly. *Housekeepers,* sometimes known as *maids,* keep hotel rooms clean. They also inspect rooms, stock linens and toiletries, and provide additional sundries, or other services, such as picking up and delivering dry cleaning for guests. In large hotels, *executive housekeepers* may supervise housekeepers and other personnel.

Maintenance and engineering workers maintain and repair the operation's equipment. They keep the electrical wiring and appliances, the plumbing, and the numerous machines in good repair and working smoothly. *Janitors* also clean the premises to attract customers, to improve safety, and to reduce wear and tear on the establishment.

DINING

In vacation settings such as spas, cruise ships, cross-country trains, and hotels and motels, food is provided to the tourists while they are in residence. The food service staff may have different titles in different locations, but essentially function as *cooks, bakers, waiters and waitresses,* and *hosts and hostesses.*

Restaurant managers and food and beverage managers direct the activities in an establishment's cocktail lounge, restaurant, and banquet facilities.

CAREERS, CONTINUED

Restaurant managers hire, train, and supervise chefs, food preparers, waiters and waitresses, dishwashers, wine stewards, buspeople, and bartenders. They deal with suppliers, make sure inventories are at their proper level, and submit daily statements on restaurant sales to the food and beverage director. The *food and beverage director* is responsible for all food and beverage services in the hotel. He or she makes decisions regarding food purchases, kitchen equipment, facility decor, and employee uniforms. They also work with restaurant and other facility managers to determine menu selections and prices. *Hotel convention service coordinators* plan and organize hotel events such as meetings, trade shows, musical performances, and wedding receptions. They work with customers to make an event successful. This may include everything from ordering flowers to arranging a menu to hiring a musical group to making sure the convention area is clean and presentable for the occasion.

ENTERTAINMENT

Spas and cruise ships also often have *entertainment directors,* who plan parties and other events and often act as hosts or hostesses. On a cruise ship, the *cruise director* oversees the staff that provides all entertainment on the ship. The entertainment staff includes *performers, movie theater workers, fitness instructors,* and any other employee who provides service to the passengers.

On large cruise ships, *cruise hosts and hostesses* handle many of the day-to-day aspects of directing the passengers to and from their entertainment activities. Some cruise lines employ hosts and hostesses to serve as *dance partners* or *escorts* to their passengers traveling alone.

Spa directors design the theme and activities and hire staff for spas. They may be the owners of the facilities as well.

EMPLOYMENT OPPORTUNITIES

The travel and hospitality industry is an important segment of society, employing millions of people and providing billions of dollars each year to the national economy. Acquiring a job within the industry depends on the job seeker's expectations, experience, qualifications, goals, and ambition.

There are opportunities in every region of the country for those who are interested in the travel branch of this industry. Tour guides and tour managers work for tour operators. Employment with tour operators may begin with a listing of major travel companies advertising for tour guides and/or managers. This list can be obtained at the office of a local travel agent. As with the

Fast Fact

other travel careers, guides and managers are advised to undertake training to hone their skills and increase productivity. Individuals who prefer to work solo within the industry may choose to go into a freelance career as either a travel specialist who advises travelers on specifics of a tour or an adventure travel outfitter.

Major airlines, such as Delta, United, American, and USAir, employ thousands of workers in various capacities. In addition, there are a number of smaller, more regional airlines that likewise offer a wide variety of employment possibilities. Rental car companies are also big employers in the travel and hospitality industry, with major companies such as Avis, Hertz, Budget, Enterprise, and Alamo operating all over the nation. There are several cruise lines, all of which hire employees to work in various capacities. Cunard, Princess, and Carnival are examples of such major cruise lines. Additionally, The National Railroad Passenger Corporation (Amtrak), which serves forty-five states and the District of Columbia, offers many employment opportunities for food and cleaning service workers, baggage porters, engineers, conductors, and others.

Most job opportunities in the hospitality branch of this industry are in highly populated areas or traditional tourist resorts, where hotel rooms are in higher demand. Lodgings in smaller towns or out-of-the-way places tend to be family-run establishments.

People interested in hotel careers may find employment with such large hotel and motel chains as Best Western International, Hilton Hotels Corporation, Hyatt Hotels Corporation, Holiday Inns, and many others. These chains may offer the best opportunities for positions in management, sales, marketing, and public relations. Some chains, such as the Host Marriott Corporation, offer "fast track" management programs designed to encourage career advancement for women and minorities, day care, and other family-friendly benefits.

INDUSTRY OUTLOOK

As one of the largest retail service industries in the United States, travel and hospitality is a booming business. In the next decade, large increases are expected in both vacation and business-related travel, making job prospects especially good. Tight competition among large and small travel companies will result in industry consolidation as the larger companies dominate the smaller. Other changes are also affecting the way the industry is structured. People are taking shorter but more frequent vacations. Three- and four-day weekends are replacing the two-week vacations that were common in the 1960s and 1970s. As the working population in the United States finds it more difficult to take extended vacations, many travel organizations have had to gear their programs around shorter trips. In addition to the growth in adventure travel, another trend is the growing popularity of ecotourism, which involves visiting a pristine natural area, learning about its ecosystem, perhaps even performing some work while there, and making every effort to preserve and protect that ecosystem without altering it by the act of traveling there. Ecotours to such places as the Galapagos Islands and Costa Rica have become very popular.

More Lingo to Learn

Hospitality industry: *The industry that umbrellas the hotel and motel, or lodging, trade. As defined by the Council on Hotel, Restaurant and Institutional Education (CHRIE), hospitality also includes food services, recreation services, and tourism.*

Niche marketing: *Hotels can attract a specific group by using special amenities and services to make foreign or special-needs-guests feel at home. Some examples are internationalized service, multilingual staff, and audio or braille hotel information and menus.*

The Red Book: *Officially known as the* Hotel and Motel Red Book. *Published yearly by the American Hotel and Motel Association, it provides a complete detailed list of lodging places in North America, Mexico, and other countries, including names of managers, officers, and affiliated industries. This can be a valuable source when job networking.*

Smart cards: *Also known as key cards, these are electronically coded plastic cards about the same size and width as a credit card. These key cards are inserted into slots located near the guest room, and if the information matches that stored at the front desk the room door will open. Cards are recoded with every new guest.*

Yet another very strong and growing segment of the industry is the cruise lines. People are opting more and more often for cruises, which offer a total vacation for a set price, and typically include several land tours in various ports of call.

While adventure travel, ecotours, and cruises are gaining in popularity, the traditional package tour is losing ground. This may be due in part to how much easier travel planning has become with increasing access to the Internet. Since a computer user can now sit at home, access almost all the necessary information about any given location, and basically plan his or her own "package tour," the demand for others to do this is lessening. This same easy access, in addition to the increasing popularity of making actual reservations online, may ultimately affect travel agencies as well. Attempting to target specific needs of a specific clientele has proven to be effective for many travel companies—with the business traveler who works for a small firm the main target. To compete with the larger travel agencies, local and regional agencies use the focus approach to attract these small businesses.

This approach is expected to result in additional careers in the industry, namely in marketing and sales.

During the early 1990s, the hotel industry suffered a severe downturn due to several reasons. A glut of new building during the 1980s created an oversupply of hotel beds. The recession of the early 1990s, coupled with the Persian Gulf War, meant people were traveling less often. When a wave of downsizing swept through American corporations, the loss of more than a million middle-management positions further reduced the levels of business travel—traditionally one of the most vital areas of the hotel industry.

However, as the economy improved toward the mid-1990s, travel, tourism, and the hotel industry in general once again enjoyed an upswing. Business travel is expected to remain steady, and even increase, despite innovations such as facsimile machines, email, and video conferencing.

International tourism, as American destinations have successfully been promoted abroad, has surged, helped by the relatively weak dollar. With large numbers of international tourists coming to the United States, hotels must learn to "internationalize" service, from international cuisine to multilingual staff people, room directories, and information. Employees knowledgeable about Japanese language and culture will especially be in demand.

More establishments will target the fast-growing elderly population, many of whom have substantial retirement funds. Called assisted living communities, these complexes will offer housing, food, and medical services. Approximately 1.5 million senior housing beds will be available in the year 2000, almost a 200 percent increase from the number of beds available today.

Consolidation will be key to growth in the future. Consortiums composed of smaller hotels and motels will pool resources and share advertising costs to edge off competition from bigger and better-known names such as Marriott and Hilton. Many larger hotels have joined with airlines, car rental agencies, and travel agents to offer complete travel packages. These businesses can present savings and convenience for travelers while increasing their name recognition and improving their business.

It has been predicted that this field will employ more people than any other industry by the next century. This industry also employs a high percentage of women and minorities compared to other industries. Occupancy rates, which had slipped to 60 percent in the early 1990s, are once again climbing. New facilities are being built, many in popular travel destinations like Las Vegas and Orlando. Though many employees in the hotel industry have worked up from unskilled, entry-level positions, advancement opportunities will be best for people with college degrees in hotel or hospitality management. It will become increasingly important to recruit skilled workers to fill new openings. The problems of finding and keeping staff are expected to become more difficult as the pool of younger workers shrinks.

Another challenge for the industry will be how it integrates new technology. Most hotels, resorts, and other organizations have already established data processing terminals to process reservations, bookkeeping procedures, and other services. Other advances include security systems based on card-activated access, in-room checkouts, and TV-based guest shopping. Those establishments that are best able to provide these and other services should be able to attract a wide range of customers. As the labor force continues to shrink, the hotel industry will increasingly automate.

The entire travel and hospitality industry is sensitive to political crises, such as terrorist acts or civil wars, and shifts in economic conditions both here and abroad. Consequently, the number of overall job opportunities fluctuates and is hard to predict. When the U.S. dollar rises, more Americans travel abroad since they are able to buy more with their dollar. Foreigners are less likely to travel to the United States when the dollar is strong because they are forced to spend more of their currency. Despite strong fluctuations in the market, it is likely that the travel and hospitality industry will remain strong for many years to come. It remains the single most important industry in many cities and regions.

WHAT DO I NEED TO KNOW ABOUT

Adventure Travel Specialist

SUMMARY

DEFINITION
Adventure travel specialists *develop, plan, and lead people on tours of places and activities that are unfamiliar to them. Most adventure travel trips involve physical participation and/or a form of environmental education.*

ALTERNATIVE JOB TITLES
Adventure outfitter
Ecotourism specialist

SALARY RANGE
$5,000 to $17,000 to $65,000+

EDUCATIONAL REQUIREMENTS
High school diploma; Bachelor's degree for some jobs

CERTIFICATION OR LICENSING
None

EMPLOYMENT OUTLOOK
About as fast as the average

HIGH SCHOOL SUBJECTS
Anthropology and Archaeology
Earth science
Geology
Geography/Social studies
Sociology

PERSONAL INTERESTS
Camping/Hiking
The Environment
Exercise/Personal fitness
Helping people: personal service
Travel

"Look directly to your left and you'll see two caribou," Steve Gilroy says to his tour group as he brings the van to a rather hurried stop. He reaches for the camera on the seat beside him. "Get your equipment together and let's walk a few yards," he says. "We should be able to get some good shots."

His ten passengers—photography buffs who have come from as far away as California to capture the Alaska experience on film—collect their cameras and film.

As they leave the van and start to walk, Steve talks to them in a low voice about the caribou. "Caribou roam constantly in search of food," he says. "They eat mostly ground lichen, plants, and the bark from small trees." He slows and lifts his camera to his eye. "In fact, we may be able to catch them digging for lichen if we're quiet."

WHAT DOES AN ADVENTURE TRAVEL SPECIALIST DO?

Depending upon where he or she works, an average day for an adventure travel specialist might be anything from planning tours in the comfort of an air-conditioned office to leading a safari through southern Africa.

Adventure travel is one of the fastest-growing areas of specialization within the travel industry. Adventure travel specialists plan—and may lead—tours of unusual, exotic, remote, or wilderness locations. Almost all adventure travel involves some physical activity that takes place outdoors. Sometimes, adventure travel is split into two different categories: soft adventure and hard adventure. Hard adventure requires a fairly high degree of commitment from participants, as well as advanced skills. A high-adventure traveler might choose to climb Yosemite's El Capitan, raft the Talkeetna River in Alaska, or mountain-bike through the logging trails in the Columbia River Gorge. Soft adventure travel, on the other hand, requires much less physical ability and is usually suitable for families. Examples of this kind of travel might be a guided horse-back ride through the Rocky Mountains, a Costa Rican wildlife-viewing tour, or a hot-air-balloon ride over Napa Valley, California.

Adventure travel specialists are the travel professionals who plan, develop, and lead these types of tours. Some work strictly in an office environment, planning trip itineraries, making reservations for transportation, activities, and lodging, and selling the tours to travelers. Others, typically called *outfitters,* work in the field, overseeing the travelers, and guiding the tour activities. In some cases, the adventure specialist both plans the logistics of the trip and guides it.

For every adventure tour that takes place, numerous plans must be made. Travelers who purchase a tour package expect to have every arrangement handled for them, from the time they arrive in the city from which the trip begins. That means that ground transportation, accommodations, and dining must all be planned and reserved. Each day's activities must also be planned in advance, and arrangements made with adventure outfitters to supply equipment and guides.

The trip planner calls lodges, hotels, or campgrounds to make reservations for the tour group and arranges ground transportation, which may be vans, buses, or jeeps, depending

Lingo to Learn

Adventure travel: *Travel away from one's local environment that includes activities adventurous to the participant.*

Ecotourism: *Travel to natural areas that conserves the environment and improves the welfare of local people.*

Hard adventure: *Activities with high levels of risk, requiring intense commitment and advanced skills.*

Nature-based tourism: *Travel away from one's local environment that includes interaction with a natural environment for education, observation, or recreation.*

Soft adventure: *Activities with a perceived risk, but low levels of actual risk, requiring minimal commitment and beginning skills; most of these activities are led by experienced guides.*

Ecotourism: Traveling Responsibly

Ecotourism is a fast-growing segment of the travel and tourism market that is often associated with adventure travel. This type of travel is defined by the Ecotourism Society as "responsible travel to natural areas which conserves the environment and improves the welfare of local people."

Ecotourism activities emphasize the goal of preserving the natural areas that tourists are visiting. They often combine outdoor recreation with learning about a region's natural history and ecology. Some ecotours even include seminars on historic or wildlife preservation or community-service projects.

upon the particular trip. He or she also works with the adventure outfitters who will actually lead the tour group through the planned activities and supply the necessary equipment.

Some companies serve as adventure travel brokers, selling both tours that they have developed and tours that have already been packaged by another company. *Travel specialists* are responsible for marketing and selling these tours. They give potential customers information about the trips offered, usually over the phone. When a customer decides to purchase a tour package, the travel specialist takes the reservation and completes any necessary paperwork. Depending upon their position in the company and their level of responsibility, adventure travel planners may decide where and how to advertise their tours.

Working as an adventure travel outfitter or guide is very different from working as an adventure travel planner or broker. The duties for these individuals vary enormously, depending upon the type of tours they lead. Adventure tours can take place on land, on water, or in the air. On a land adventure trip, guides may take their tour groups rock climbing, caving, mountain biking, wilderness hiking, horseback riding, or wildlife viewing. On a water trip, they may go snorkeling, scuba diving, surfing, kayaking, whitewater rafting, or canoeing. Air adventures include skydiving, parasailing, hang gliding, bungee jumping, and hot air ballooning.

Whatever the nature of the trip, guides are responsible for overseeing the group members' activities and ensuring their safety. They may demonstrate activities, help with equipment, or assist a group member who is having difficulty. In many cases, where travelers are interested in the scenery, geography, wildlife, or history of a location, guides serve as commentators, explaining the unique aspects of the region as the group travels.

Guides are also responsible for helping tour group members in the case of an emergency or unplanned event. Depending upon the nature of their tour, they must be prepared to deal with injuries, dangerous situations, and unusual and unplanned happenings. Essentially, it is the guide's responsibility to ensure that tour group members have a safe, memorable, and enjoyable trip.

WHAT IS IT LIKE TO BE AN ADVENTURE TRAVEL SPECIALIST?

Steve Gilroy is a professional photographer who has turned his love of the Alaskan outdoors into a second career—that of photography tour guide. Each year, his company, Alaska Photo Tours, takes approximately 120 photography buffs on tours of the Alaskan countryside, allowing them to capture spectacular scenery and wildlife on film.

"We offer custom trips for small groups that put people into great photographic situations," he says. "It's for people who like taking pictures and who don't want to be caught in a huge tour group or be in the really touristy places." Steve's trips begin in either Anchorage or Juneau, Alaska, and last seven to twelve days. His tour groups are small, with no more than eleven travelers. He plans every detail of each of the company's twelve yearly trips, and serves as a guide on about half of them.

Steve begins planning a trip more than eighteen months in advance. With attention to every detail, he plans tours that will take travelers to the right places at the right times of the year for the best photographic opportunities. "We dictate the schedule around the wildlife and the scenery," he says. "I only travel at the best times." Long before the tour ever begins, he has reserved lodging, any in-state flights, natural history guides for certain locations, and even private rooms in restaurants.

❝❝I give them a plan of attack and tell them what the next day's goals are. I'll say 'we're hoping to see whales tomorrow . . . or we're going to see if we can get a bald eagle to swoop down by the boat.'❞

At the beginning of a tour, after collecting all of his travelers from the airport, Steve conducts an orientation meeting, and discusses the coming day's activities. "I give them a plan of attack and tell them what the next day's goals are," he says. "I'll say 'we're hoping to see whales tomorrow . . . or we're going to see if we can get a bald eagle to swoop down by the boat.' I try to give them some expectation of what we might see."

Steve's tours usually consist of a segment in coastal Alaska, one near Mount McKinley, and one in his hometown of Talkeetna to give travelers a taste of life in rural Alaska. "Most visitors want a balanced trip," he says. "So this way, they get to see the glaciers, sea otters, whales, and puffins of coastal Alaska, plus the grandeur of Mount McKinley and the grizzlies, caribou, moose, wolves, and tundra." The tour group usually spends between three and five days in each location.

Steve takes his tour groups out into the Alaska landscape to look for photographic opportunities. When touring on land, they travel in a fifteen-passenger luxury van, which makes periodic stops at likely locations. "We take short hikes, with vehicle support," he says. "We'll stop, gather our equipment, and go for a short walk because I know of good photo opportunities in the area, or we've spotted an animal."

During each of the visitors' hikes, Steve educates them on their surroundings. "As we walk, I give them background on the wildlife, what to look for, how to approach," he says. "It's important to me to share the whole Alaska experience . . . vegetation, wildlife, natural history." He also advises group members on how to stay safe in the unfamiliar territory. "I always tell them what to be careful of," he says. "I tell them about bear behaviors, how to walk on the lumpy tundra so that they don't twist an ankle, that sort of thing." All of the guides on Steve's tours are required to be trained in first aid and CPR.

Steve often contracts with a local flight service company to take his groups on aerial tours of Mount McKinley. Some tours also include short cruises off the coast in *Zodiacs*—motorized rubber skiffs. "This allows us to go ashore, to walk a beach littered with car-sized icebergs, to go into a meadow where the wildflowers are gorgeous," Steve says. The goal is a photographic exploration of Alaska.

HAVE I GOT WHAT IT TAKES TO BE AN ATS?

A love of the outdoors is perhaps the most important characteristic of travel specialists who work in the field. "People who enter this career are the kind of people who just naturally spend their free time outdoors," says Steve. "So, they grew up hiking and fishing and camping . . . and that love of outdoors just carried them to the point where they decided to combine their love of nature with their career." Steve says that it's also important for adventure travel tour guides to have a passion for sharing their love of nature and their knowledge with others.

An educational background in the natural sciences is important for some adventure travel guides; for others, a high skill level in certain activities, such as rock climbing or cross-country skiing, is necessary. Whatever type of tours you guide, however, being in reasonably good physical shape is a must.

Steve also says that being mature and responsible is important in this sort of job, where you are leading groups of people through areas and activities unfamiliar to them. "Common sense is really important," he says. "You have to be ready to respond if something unplanned happens." Guides should be trained and confident in performing emergency first aid and CPR.

To be a successful adventure travel specialist, you should:

Enjoy spending time outdoors

Be responsible and able to think on your feet

Be detail-oriented

Communicate well with others

Be in good physical condition

Know emergency first aid and CPR

Adventure travel professionals who work in an office, developing and selling tours, need some different personal qualities than those who work in the field. Dave Wiggins, who owns one of the nation's oldest adventure travel brokerages, says that he looks for people with a good work ethic. "You can train someone to do everything else, but you can't teach the right attitude."

Dave says that it's also important to be friendly and confident, and to have good phone skills. "We look for people with a good head on their shoulders who can speak intelligently about the different programs we sell," he says. While being an active, outdoorsy person may help you sell tours, it is not a requirement for working in this branch of adventure travel. According to Dave, attention to detail and good organizational skills are more significant.

HOW DO I BECOME AN ADVENTURE TRAVEL SPECIALIST?

Because the field of adventure travel is so wide and varied, the possible educational paths leading to it are numerous. Steve, for example, holds two college degrees, has traveled the world extensively, and has been a professional photographer for thirteen years. On the other end of the spectrum, Dave Wiggins says that having a college degree is less important than having customer relations or sales experience. Whatever type of adventure travel you hope to work in, however, you can start to prepare for it now.

EDUCATION

High School
If you are considering the business end of travel—working in a brokerage, planning tours, or eventually owning your own tour-packaging business, you should start taking business courses while still in high school. Accounting, computer science, mathematics, or any other business-related course will give

you a good start. Classes in geography, geology, social studies, and history might also help you understand and discuss the locations you may be dealing with. Finally, classes in English or speech are always good choices for helping you develop the ability and confidence to deal with people.

If you are more interested in the fieldwork aspect of adventure travel, you will need to take classes that help you understand how the Earth's environment and ecosystem work. Because tour guides often explain the natural history of a location, or educate tour groups on local wildlife and plant life, classes in earth science, biology, and geology are excellent choices. Classes that teach you about the social history of various places—such as social studies or anthropology—might also be beneficial.

Since much adventure travel involves physical activity, which may range from low- to high-impact, taking courses or becoming involved in activities that promote physical fitness is a good idea. If you already have an interest in a particular area of adventure travel, you may be able to join clubs or take classes that help you develop the right skills. For example, scuba diving, sailing, hiking, mountain biking, canoeing, and fishing are all adventure travel activities that you might be able to engage in while still in high school.

Postsecondary Training

There are several different approaches you can take to prepare for a career in adventure travel. While it may not be necessary for all jobs, a college degree will likely give you a competitive edge in most employment situations. If you choose to obtain a college degree, some options for majors might be earth science, biology, geology, natural history, or environmental affairs. If you hope to become involved with an intensely physical form of adventure travel, a degree in health, physical education, or recreation may be a good choice.

If you are more interested in the planning and reservations end of adventure travel, a college degree in business is a good choice. Some adventure travel brokers suggest that attending one of the many travel agent schools also provides a good background for the administrative aspects of the business.

It may be possible to find a job in adventure travel without college training, if you happen to be very experienced and skilled in some form of adventure activity. If you choose this path, you should spend as much time as possible developing whatever skill you are interested in. There are classes, clubs, and groups that can teach you anything from beginning diving to advanced rock climbing.

WHO WILL HIRE ME?

In the last five years, there has been an enormous increase in the number of adventure travel providers. In addition to this growth in commercial suppliers, a number of not-for-profit organizations—such as universities and environmental groups—are also offering nature and adventure programs.

Your first step in finding a job should be to develop a list of American and Canadian adventure travel wholesalers and outfitters; you might talk to a travel agent or check with the reference desk of your local library. Another option is to hop on the Web and perform a keyword search on "adventure travel" or "outfitters." Many of these organizations have their own Web sites.

There are a number of magazines that may be helpful in compiling a list. Some good publications to look into are *Outside, Backpacker,* and *Bicycling.* A final method of getting a list of travel wholesalers and outfitters is to contact one or all of the adventure travel organizations listed at the end of this book. These associations should be able to give you a list of their members.

To find not-for-profit organizations that hire adventure travel specialists, consider the National Audubon Society and the Sierra Club. Again, check with your local library for a more complete listing of environmental groups. You might also contact universities to see if they have a wilderness/adventure travel division in their schools of physical education or recreation.

Once you have a list of adventure travel companies, you may need to do some research to discover what sort of activities their tours consist of. That way, you can narrow your search to companies that specialize in the activity or activities you are experienced in. Remember that for your best chance of finding a job in adventure travel, you may have to relocate, so your search should be geographically broad. After you've chosen the companies to which you will apply, you should either send a resume and cover letter directly to each company or make a preliminary phone call to inquire about possibilities.

You should also use any contacts you have—from clubs, organizations, previous travel experiences, or college classes—to find out about possible employment opportunities. If you belong to a diving or bicycling club, for example, be sure to ask other members or instructors if they are familiar with any outfitters you could contact. If you have dealt with outfitters in some of your own adventure trips, you might contact them for potential job leads.

WHERE CAN I GO FROM HERE?

There is no clearly defined career path for adventure travel specialists. For those who work in an office environment, advancement will likely take the form of increased responsibility and higher pay. Assuming a managerial role or moving on to a larger company are other advancement possibilities.

For those who work in the field, advancement might mean taking more trips per year. Adventure travel in many locations is seasonal, and therefore, tour guides may not be able to do this sort of work year-round. It is not uncommon for an individual to guide tours only part-time, and have another job to fill in the slow times. If a tour guide were to become experienced in two or more particular areas of travel, however, he or she might be able to spend more, or even all, of the year doing adventure touring.

Another option for either the office worker or the guide would be to learn about the other side of the business. With experience in all aspects of developing, selling, and leading tours, the ambitious travel specialist might be able to own his or her own company. "You could become your own tour operator in an area that you know and love," says Steve, "which is what I've done."

WHAT ARE SOME RELATED JOBS?

The work of adventure travel specialists has not yet been classified by the U.S. Department of Labor. The office work of an adventure travel specialist is similar in nature to that of a *travel agent* (classified by the Department of Labor under the heading, Sales Occupations, Transportation Services); a *reservation agent* (classified by the Department of Labor under the heading, Accommodation Clerks and Gate and Ticket Agents); and a *tour operator* or *tour guide* (classified by the Department of Labor under the heading, Guides). Other careers that are related to adventure travel specialists include tour operators, airport guides, flight attendants, passenger ship stewards and stewardesses, crew schedulers, hosts and hostesses, alpine guides, and sight-seeing guides.

Related Jobs

Airport guides

Alpine guides

Crew schedulers

Flight attendants

Hosts and hostesses

Reservation agents

Ship stewards and stewardesses

Sight-seeing guides

Tour guides

Tour managers

Tour operators

WHAT ARE THE SALARY RANGES?

There is very little information available on what adventure travel specialists earn. Those who work in the field may find that they have peak and slack times of the year that correspond to destination weather conditions or vacation and travel seasons.

According to one Canadian university that offers a two-year degree in adventure travel guiding, program graduates make between $125 and $225 per day, or about $17,000 for a three- to four-month guiding season. Tour guides and tour planners in other areas of travel than adventure may make anywhere from $9.75 to $20.00 per hour. Experienced guides with managerial responsibilities can earn up to $65,000 per year, including tips.

Adventure travel specialists who work in the field generally receive free meals and accommodations while on tour, and often receive a set amount of money per day to cover other expenses. Major tour packagers and outfitters may offer their employees a fringe benefits package, including sick pay, health insurance, and pension plans.

WHAT IS THE JOB OUTLOOK?

More than half of all U.S. traveling adults, or about 73 million people, have taken an adventure trip in their lifetime, according to the U.S. Travel Data Center. Of these 73 million, about three-fourths have taken an adventure trip in the last two years. This indicates that the market for adventure travel is quite large, and is likely growing.

Many trends in today's society indicate that this growth is likely to continue. One reason is that the public's awareness and interest in physical health is growing; this leads more and more people to pursue physical activities as a form of recreation. Another reason is that as more people realize that a healthy environment means a better quality of life, there is an increased interest in wildlife and wilderness issues. Adventure travel often encompasses both physical activity and education on and preservation of natural areas, so it is a natural choice for many travelers.

On a more general note, there is a projected increase in *all* forms of travel. As the cost of travel decreases, and incomes increase, more and more people are finding it possible to take vacations. This increase in travel in general should be reflected in the adventure segment of the industry.

Despite the general growth in the field, however, it should be noted that jobs as tour guides may not be easy to come by. Compared to the rest of the travel market, the adventure segment is still fairly small. Perhaps more significantly, tour guide positions are considered very desirable. According to Dave Wiggins, job openings for field work in adventure travel are somewhat limited and highly sought-after. "There are outfitters out there who get maybe five hundred applications a year," he says. "And they can hire maybe two new people."

Flight Attendant

SUMMARY

DEFINITION
Flight attendants *help airline passengers have a safe and comfortable flight. They prepare the cabin for passenger boarding, help passengers stow luggage and find their seats, and demonstrate the use of emergency equipment. During flight, they serve drinks and prepared snacks or meals, and try to make passengers as comfortable as possible. At the end of a flight, attendants help passengers retrieve their luggage and leave the plane.*

ALTERNATIVE JOB TITLES
Steward
Stewardess

SALARY RANGE
$12,800 to $29,600 to $40,000

EDUCATIONAL REQUIREMENTS
High school diploma

CERTIFICATION OR LICENSING
None

EMPLOYMENT OUTLOOK
Faster than the average

HIGH SCHOOL SUBJECTS
Foreign language
Psychology
Speech

PERSONAL INTERESTS
Helping people: personal service
Travel

It is a Friday evening flight to Dallas and, as is typical, the plane is at full capacity. Tired business travelers on their way home from meetings read newspapers or work on their laptop computers. Excited vacationers, flying in for a week or a weekend getaway, chatter about their plans for fun and adventure.

For Sandy Teichman, taking drink orders near the back of the cabin, it is just a routine flight until she notices the young boy in the aisle seat who is having trouble breathing.

"Honey, are you okay?" she asks, pausing in her rounds to kneel beside him. The boy shakes his head, obviously frightened. His breathing is growing increasingly raspy and he is beginning to turn pale.

Sandy motions another flight attendant to her, and speaks in a low voice so as not to alarm the boy or the other passengers. "Michael, go tell the pilot we may have a problem with a passenger here. Let him know there's a chance we may have to divert." As Michael walks quickly toward the cockpit, Sandy releases the oxygen mask from the compartment over the boy's head. "Sweetheart, I'm going to put this on you for a minute and see if it helps you breathe, okay?" she says, still speaking quietly. "Don't be scared."

35

WHAT DOES A FLIGHT ATTENDANT DO?

Flight attendants attend to the safety and comfort of airline passengers from the time they board the plane until they leave it. Attendants are usually assigned to a base, which is one of the large cities that their airline flies into and out of. Full-time flight attendants fly approximately eighty hours each month, and spend another eighty on the ground, preparing planes for flight, writing reports on completed flights, and waiting for planes that arrive late. Attendants work long days, but overall, they have more days off than employees in standard nine-to-five jobs.

The attendants' responsibilities begin about an hour before the plane takes off, when they report to a briefing session with the rest of the flight crew. At the briefing session, they receive information about weather conditions that may affect the flight and passengers who may have special needs.

Before passengers board the plane, flight attendants check emergency equipment to make sure it is in working order; ensure that the passenger cabins are clean, orderly, and stocked with pillows and blankets; and check the airplane kitchens, or galleys, to make sure that they are supplied with enough food and drinks for the flight.

As passengers board the plane, attendants greet them and help them stow their luggage and coats and find their seats. They may have to give special assistance to passengers who are elderly, disabled, or traveling with small children. Before takeoff, a flight attendant uses a loudspeaker to address the passengers. He or she welcomes them to their flight and gives them any necessary information about delays, weather conditions, or flight times. As required by federal law, the flight attendants demonstrate how to use the plane's emergency equipment, and check to make sure all passenger seat backs are in upright position and all seat belts are fastened before takeoff.

During the flight, attendants usually serve passengers drinks and either meals or snacks, depending upon the time and the length of the flight. They may also pass out magazines, newspapers, headphones, or pil-

Lingo to Learn

Bulkhead: *The walls on an airplane that divide the cabin into sections.*

Cabin: *The passenger compartment of an airplane.*

FAA: *Federal Aviation Administration, government body that regulates safety standards for aircraft and aviation personnel.*

Flight deck: *Also called the cockpit, the area of the plane where the pilot and copilot sit.*

Galley: *An airplane kitchen.*

Hub: *A city or an airport in which an airline has major operations and many gates.*

Leg: *One complete flight, from takeoff to landing.*

Minimum Equipment List (MEL): *A list of aircraft equipment that must be in good working order before an aircraft can legally take off with passengers.*

Pressurized aircraft: *An aircraft that is kept at a designated atmospheric pressure so that passengers can breathe normally.*

Turbulence: *Rough, sometimes violent, atmospheric conditions encountered by airplanes.*

lows and blankets to passengers. They may answer questions, help entertain children, or control unruly passengers. Taking care of passengers who are sick or frightened is another important part of the flight attendant's job.

Although they may never encounter an air emergency, it is very important for flight attendants to know what to do should one occur. In the event of an emergency evacuation, attendants must help passengers leave the plane in a rapid, safe, and orderly fashion. They may have to open emergency doors and inflate emergency slides to allow passengers to evacuate.

After the plane lands, flight attendants help passengers retrieve their luggage from overhead compartments and leave the plane. On international flights, they may provide customs and airport information and sometimes translate flight information or instructions into a foreign language for passengers. When all the passengers have left the plane, flight attendants tidy the cabin, picking up trash and straightening seat belts before the next flight.

Attendants may also have some clerical duties. They may collect and account for money made on liquor sales, file incident reports, and fill out forms relating to liquor inventory, lost and found items, or cabin maintenance.

WHAT IS IT LIKE TO BE A FLIGHT ATTENDANT?

Sandy Teichman is what you might call a frequent flyer. As a flight attendant for Southwest Airlines, in fact, she has probably logged more air miles than even the most dedicated business or enthusiastic leisure traveler. And that's just fine with her. "I just enjoy it so much," she says. "It's a great career for anyone."

Sandy's work day starts either at 5:00 in the morning or 2:00 in the afternoon, depending upon which shift she is working. "We have morning trips from around 6:00 AM to 2:00 PM, and we have afternoon trips from around 3:00 to 11:00 PM." An average shift consists of six legs—or individual flights—between airports. The shift ends in an "overnight," Sandy says, when the flight attendants and pilots go off duty until the next day when they report for another shift. Depending upon which flights the attendant is working, his or her overnight could be in any number of destination cities. Therefore, the flight attendant, along with the rest of the crew, spends the night in a hotel.

"When you get off your shift, the van is there at the airport to take you to your hotel," Sandy says. "And usually on your van ride, you turn to your crew and ask 'What do you want to do?'" Sandy says that she and her co-workers usually meet for dinner and perhaps shopping or sightseeing. If she is working the morning shift, she usually makes it an early night, however, since she must report to the airport at 5:00 the following morning.

There are three flight attendants for each flight, and they each have specific positions. Before passengers board, there are some preliminary tasks to attend to. The three attendants check the kitchens, or galleys, to make sure they are adequately stocked, check the lavatories, check the emergency equipment, and do a security check. When the passengers start to board, the flight attendants assume their positions: one in the front of the plane, one in the middle by the emergency window exit, and one at the back. "The front person stays at the front of the plane and greets passengers," says Sandy. "The back two help put baggage up and generally monitor the whole boarding process." According to Federal Aviation Administration regulations, the attendants must make sure that all passengers are seated and all carry-on baggage is properly stowed before the plane pushes back from the gate.

As the plane leaves the gate, the front flight attendant explains the safety procedures over the intercom, while the back two attendants demonstrate them to the passengers. Before the plane actually takes off, they sit down and remain seated until they reach a certain altitude.

"As soon as we can, we get up and start serving," says Sandy. "After everyone has been served, we go back through to see if anyone needs seconds or thirds and to pick up trash." In addition to these specific duties, the flight attendants are responsible for helping passengers with any questions or problems they might have and generally trying to make their flight a comfortable and enjoyable one. This may include passing out pillows and blankets, providing passengers with reading material, and helping comfort any passenger who is frightened or ill.

Sandy says that helping sick passengers is a big part of the job. "When you're going through flight attendant training, you don't realize how often you'll use first aid," she says. "It's not all that uncommon to have someone who's having difficulty breathing or who's having chest pains. And of course, some people get airsick." She also frequently deals with passengers who are afraid to fly or who panic if the flight is rough.

Once the plane has landed and taxied to the gate, the flight attendants help the passengers retrieve their luggage from the overhead compartments and exit the plane. Then they clean up the cabin for the next flight. This includes picking up any trash left behind by the passengers and making sure all the seat belts are straightened. On the last leg of the shift, before the attendants go off duty, they must make an accounting of any money they have collected for drinks, and drop this off at the airline office. They also speak briefly with the new flight attendants coming on duty to pass on any information they might need to know about the cabin or the galleys.

HAVE I GOT WHAT IT TAKES TO BE A FLIGHT ATTENDANT?

Sandy feels that being responsible and compassionate are two of the most important characteristics of a good flight attendant. "A flight attendant should be the kind of person you'd want to put your grandmother on a plane with because you know they'd take care of her," she says. According to Sandy, it's also important to be able to assert yourself while still being tactful. "You might have someone who's had too much to drink—that happens sometimes on evening flights," she says. "It takes a special kind of person to go out there and handle that situation. You need to not be afraid to confront someone, but to be able to control *how* you confront them."

Flexibility is also an important personality trait for flight attendants, Sandy says, because bad weather and delayed flights can change your plans at the last minute. "It doesn't happen too often, but occasionally if there's bad weather, your flight might get rerouted and you might not end up in the city you planned on, or at the time you planned on," she says. "That can be irritating, but you have to know that it can happen."

It is important that flight attendants be able to deal effectively with any sort of crisis or emergency situation. Passengers depend on them for help in any situation that arises, whether it be something as minor as airsickness or as major as an emergency evacuation of the plane. "You've got to have someone who can deal with stress, who can keep themselves under control and not freak out," says Sandy. "When someone's sick or scared on a plane, you're the one they turn to."

Because they are on their feet for most of their working hours, flight attendants need a certain level of stamina. Sandy says that although the job was tiring at first, she got used to it quickly. "You just have to work yourself up to being able to stand on your feet like that," she says. Because the job does require a certain level of energy and endurance, most airlines require

To be a successful flight attendant, you should:

Be neat and well groomed

Have physical stamina

Enjoy dealing with people

Be poised, confident, and articulate

Have a warm, outgoing, and compassionate personality

Be controlled, level-headed, and able to respond properly in an emergency

that their flight attendants pass a medical examination and meet certain height and weight standards.

Finally, flight attendants must be willing to accept a slightly different lifestyle than most jobs require. They may be scheduled to work nights, weekends, and on holidays, and they may be away from home for several days at a time. However, because their shifts are longer than the standard eight hours, flight attendants work only three to four days a week.

One aspect of the job that appeals to many is the opportunity to travel. "As corny as it sounds, it's a chance to get out and see parts of the world that you never would be able to see otherwise," Sandy says. "It truly is a rewarding and great job."

HOW DO I BECOME A FLIGHT ATTENDANT?

EDUCATION

High School

Although many airlines prefer to hire applicants with some college experience, a high school diploma is the minimum educational requirement for this job. Start taking courses that build your communication skills. A flight attendant serves to represent his or her airline to its passengers, so airlines want attendants who can speak clearly and professionally. Poor English, grammar, or enunciation may disqualify an applicant. To enhance these skills you should focus on English and speech classes. Classes in a foreign language are also good choices, since international airlines usually require their flight attendants to be fluent in a second language.

Because so much of the flight attendant's job involves dealing with people, courses in psychology may be helpful. A psychology background may prove especially helpful in dealing with passengers who are frightened or upset. Finally, classes in geography and sociology could help familiarize you with the places to which you may travel as a flight attendant.

Aside from choosing classes with an eye toward the future, you can begin to prepare for a career as a flight attendant by finding a summer or part-time job that allows you to work with the public. Jobs in customer service or customer relations are very helpful, according to Sandy. "If someone has had customer service experience, they'll almost certainly be invited in for a group interview," she says.

Postsecondary Training

Because many airlines prefer to hire employees with some college experience, it is advisable to complete a two-year or four-year college degree. Although there is no specific major that will prepare you for a career as a flight attendant, degrees in psychology, public speaking, and nurse's aid training are all good choices. A business degree with an emphasis in customer service or public relations is another excellent option. If you are especially interested in international flights, you might consider getting a foreign language degree.

Regardless of their previous education, all flight attendants are required by their airlines to complete a four- to six-week training course. While most large airlines maintain their own schools for flight attendants, some of the smaller airlines may not. These smaller companies often send their flight attendants to schools run by the larger carriers.

During an airline training program, flight attendants learn how to respond in an emergency. They are taught how to administer first aid, how to use the airplane's oxygen system, and how to evacuate the plane in an emergency. Sandy says that Southwest flight attendant training focuses heavily on these elements. "We have a simulated plane that is on hydraulics, and we simulate a plane crash," she says. "You have to go through the steps of sitting there, hearing the crash, and jumping up and performing the evacuation. We even have theatrical smoke that fills the plane."

Attendants also learn the basics of customer service, grooming requirements, FAA regulations, company operations and schedules, aircraft equipment, and how to fill out flight report forms. Airlines also train attendants in public relations policies. "They teach you how to deal with delicate situations, like if someone has had a death in the family," she says. "They teach you how to deal with wheelchairs and guide dogs. Basically, they train you in all the different kinds of situations you might encounter on the job."

Trainees for international flights are taught how to deal with customs and visa regulations, and what to do in the event of a terrorist attack. Near the end of the training program, attendants go on practice flights, in which they perform their duties under supervision. Once they have completed the initial training period, flight attendants must have twelve to fourteen hours of additional training in emergency procedures each year, as mandated by the FAA.

LABOR UNIONS

Most flight attendants belong to one of three labor unions: the Association of Flight Attendants, the Transport Workers Union of America, or the

International Brotherhood of Teamsters. In exchange for the weekly or monthly payment of dues, flight attendants who belong to one of these unions receive a package of services designed to improve the working environment. Union services often include collective bargaining for pay and benefits, governmental lobbying, and legal representation.

WHO WILL HIRE ME?

Sandy was working as a secretary in a large company when she first became interested in the aviation industry. "One of the men I worked with, his wife was a flight attendant for Southwest," she says. "She really liked it and I thought it sounded like fun, so she got me an application." Sandy started her career with Southwest as a reservation agent. After three and a half years in reservations, she decided to switch departments and become a flight attendant.

The best way to start a job search for this position is to compile a list of all major airlines, and contact their personnel departments directly. Although you may be familiar with many of these airlines—such as American, USAir, United, Delta, Continental—there are many others that are smaller or particular to a certain region of the United States. For a complete list of domestic airlines, contact the Air Transport Association of America.

Once you have obtained a complete list, send your resume, along with a cover letter, to each airline you are interested in. Also, many airlines have offices on the premises of major airports. If you are near such an airport, you might consider visiting the airlines' offices to talk with representatives; it may be possible to apply for a position in this manner.

Some of the major airlines have personnel recruiting teams that travel through the country, interviewing prospective flight attendants. Airline company offices can provide you with information about these recruitment visits, which are sometimes announced in newspaper advertisements as well.

Although the vast majority of flight attendants are employed by commercial airlines, there are a small number who work for private companies. Many large corporations, such as IBM, 3M, or Exxon, maintain their own aircraft for the purpose of flying their executives from place to place. One or more flight attendants may be present on these jets, depending upon the size. Because most corporations prefer to hire experienced flight attendants, however, finding a job in a private company is unlikely for the beginning attendant.

WHERE CAN I GO FROM HERE?

Sandy plans to become a flight attendant supervisor. In this position, she will spend most of her time in the airline's offices, overseeing other flight attendants and working with the scheduling and payroll departments. She says that there are several other advancement possibilities for flight attendants within the in-flight department as well. "It's very rare that I see flight attendants change departments," she says. "They can become trainers or they can become managers or directors who work directly over the flight attendants, or they can become interviewers or recruiters." Some attendants combine the best of both worlds by spending part of their time working flights and part of their time in the office.

When a flight attendant is new, he or she is placed on reserve status. Reserve attendants do not have a regular schedule; rather, they must be available on short notice to work extra flights or to fill in for attendants who are sick or on vacation. It may take an attendant between one and five years to move out of reserve status, depending upon the number of flight attendants in his or her airline who retire, leave the job, or are promoted.

When the attendant is promoted out of reserve status, he or she may bid on regular assignments for airline bases or flight schedules. Because these assignments are made on the basis of seniority, the longer the attendant has been employed, the more likely it is that he or she will receive an assignment of choice.

There are several opportunities for further advancement as well. Flight attendants may advance to first flight attendant (sometimes also called flight purser), supervising flight attendant, instructor, or airline recruitment representative.

Advancement possibilities

Flight attendant supervisors oversee other flight attendants and monitor their performance, serve as a liaison between attendants and airline scheduling and payroll departments, and interview applicants for open positions.

Flight attendant instructors train new flight attendants on aircraft specifications, FAA regulations, emergency procedures, customer service, and first aid; and conduct refresher training courses for flight attendants already employed.

Flight attendant recruiters may travel around the country to interview prospective applicants for flight attendant positions, represent their airline at career or job fairs, and visit high schools or college campuses to meet with interested students.

WHAT ARE SOME RELATED JOBS?

The job of flight attendant basically consists of serving airline passengers, and ensuring that they have a safe and smooth flight. This type of work is similar in nature to several other positions in both the transportation industry and the service industry, including concierges, cruise directors, reservation and transportation ticket agents, tour guides, and travel agents.

The U.S. Department of Labor classifies flight attendants under the heading, Workers in Safety and Comfort Services. Other workers in this group include ramp attendants, passenger service representatives, bus attendants, funeral attendants, brakers on passenger trains, Pullman conductors, and ship stewards and stewardesses.

The U.S. Department of Labor also classifies flight attendants with hostesses and hosts and stewardesses and stewards. Also in this category are social directors of cruise ships, waiters and waitresses in private clubs, airline lounge receptionists, and bus attendants.

WHAT ARE THE SALARY RANGES?

The average salary for all flight attendants in the late 1990s was $29,600 per year, with senior flight attendants earning as much as $35,000 to $40,000 per year. Beginning attendants, however, earned only around $12,800, according to the Association of Flight Attendants. Wage and work schedule requirements are established by union contract.

Most attendants receive a base pay for a certain number of flight hours each month. They then receive extra pay for overtime and night flights. FAA regulations limit the number of flying hours attendants can work per week, however, so there is a cap on overtime hours. Many airlines pay more for international flights than for domestic ones.

Almost all airlines pay attendants' expenses such as food, ground transportation, and overnight lodging when they are on duty away from home. Most airlines require their flight attendants to wear uniforms. Some airlines require new attendants to purchase their own; others supply the uniforms at no cost.

Flight attendants typically receive a standard benefits package, which includes paid sick and vacation time, free or reduced air fare for themselves and family members, and in some cases, medical and life insurance and a pension plan.

Related Jobs
Airline lounge receptionists
Brakers on passenger trains
Bus attendants
Concierges
Cruise directors
Customer service representative
Funeral attendants
Host/Hostess
Passenger service representatives
Pullman conductors
Ramp attendants
Reservation and transportation ticket agents
Ship stewards and stewardesses
Social directors of cruise ships
Tour guides
Travel agents
Wait persons

WHAT IS THE JOB OUTLOOK?

Job prospects for this career are expected to be good in the coming several years, with employment of flight attendants predicted to grow faster than the average for all occupations through the year 2006. The main reason for this growth is an increase in the number of people who are flying. As more efficient aircraft and competition between airlines have caused a decrease in air fares, flying has become a more economically feasible means of traveling for many people. This increase in air traffic is expected to continue; some estimates say that the number of people flying will increase more than 60 percent in the coming decade. To accommodate the growing number of passengers, airlines are using larger aircraft and scheduling more flights. Since FAA regulations require one flight attendant for every fifty passengers aboard a plane, there should be a heightened need for these workers.

Job openings will also arise from the need to replace flight attendants who get promoted, leave the field, or switch departments.

Even with the growing need for attendants, however, there is keen competition for these positions. Airlines receive thousands of applications from prospective flight attendants each year, so you will have the best chance of finding a job in this field if you have at least two years of college and some prior work experience in dealing with the public.

Although the job outlook for flight attendants is expected to be good, it is important to be aware that the airline industry is very sensitive to the overall state of the nation's economy. During economic downturns, people cut back on their leisure travel and many businesses reduce their business travel as well. When the demand for air travel declines, full-time flight attendants may be put on part-time status or laid off, and very few new attendants are hired.

Hotel Concierge

SUMMARY

DEFINITION
The concierge is the hotel's best representative for guest services. They provide services to help make the guest's hotel stay more enjoyable. They offer recommendations regarding the city's best restaurants, shows, museums, and tours. Concierges can also book flights and arrange car or limousine rentals.

ALTERNATIVE JOB TITLES
Guest service representative

SALARY REQUIREMENTS
$25,000 to $35,000 to $50,000

EDUCATIONAL REQUIREMENTS
High school diploma

CERTIFICATION OR LICENSING
None. Membership in the association, Les Clefs d'Or, is highly desirable.

EMPLOYMENT OUTLOOK
Faster than the average

HIGH SCHOOL SUBJECTS
Art
English (writing/literature)
Foreign language
History
Speech

PERSONAL INTERESTS
Helping people: emotionally
Helping people: personal service
Music
Psychology
Reading/Books
Theater

"Can you tell me how to get to the Golden Gate Bridge?" an elderly couple asks.

Diana Nelson searches a neat stack of colored cards, and hands them a preprinted direction card to the famous San Francisco landmark. "Here you go," she says, smiling. "Make sure you stop at Golden Gate Park. That's the best place for taking photos." The couple thanks her for the suggestion and depart for a day of sightseeing.

Almost immediately another hotel guest comes to the concierge desk. "I left my laptop computer in the trunk of the taxi," the harried guest moans. "I have a noon deadline to meet. Can you help me?" Without hesitation, Diana makes a quick call to the hotel's business center and secures a portable computer to loan the guest for the day. "Can you remember the name of the taxi company, or the driver's name, perhaps? Where did the cab pick you up?" Diana keeps a computer listing of all taxi companies in town and after a few phone calls she is able to track down the missing laptop, much to the relief of the hotel guest.

Diana spends the rest of her afternoon sorting through the stacks of requests for airline tickets and car rentals. Since Diana knows of a rental car company that is especially trustworthy, she knows her guests receive the best deal available. Her assistant spends a good two hours making airline reservations, consulting the *Official Airline Guide* (the handbook for booking and reserving flights) on more than one occasion.

It's almost six o'clock in the evening—Diana and her staff, after a busy day with over two hundred requests to tackle, are more than ready to head home. Just then the phone rings. "Hello, this is Mr. Ishmael, in Suite 2424. I'm sorry for the short notice, but I need to entertain about twenty clients tonight, in my room. Nothing much. Drinks, dinner, etc. Will you take care of it for me? Oh yes, I'd like to have live music . . ."

"Of course," Diana replies, turning to the computerized files for small jazz ensembles. Magic is about to happen.

WHAT DOES A CONCIERGE DO?

Concierges are the most visible and active ambassadors of hotel hospitality. Their basic duty is to provide hotel guests with services to help make their hotel stay as comfortable, enjoyable, and memorable as possible. Concierges are often compared to magicians because they are able to procure the most basic or the most outrageous request—from airline reservations to hard-to-get concert tickets.

The Genesis of the Concierge

Concierges have been around since the Middle Ages. The term concierge is derived from the Latin term conservus, meaning "fellow slave." In the past, certain slaves were trained to assist their owners, often traveling ahead to make sure accommodations and food were in order. Holding the keys to the castle, these slaves became doorkeepers; and they were trusted to make sure everyone was safely locked in for the night. Throughout the years, as luxury hotels were built across Europe, it was necessary to install concierges to provide the same type of service for their guests.

Although they have long been mainstays of many European hotels, it was not until the mid-1970s that concierges became more prevalent in the United States. Today, concierges are found mostly in large urban hotels. Their offices range from massive counters equal to the front desk in size, or small niches arranged in one corner of the hotel lobby. Most often, they are found behind a large desk in the lobby, near the front desk. Armed with their computers, rolodexes, and telephones, concierges are available to all hotel guests.

Many of the requests concierges receive are very basic, such as directions to city attractions, recommendations to tours or restaurants, or help dealing with airlines or car rental agencies. Concierges can take care of tasks such as obtaining out-of-town newspapers, dry cleaning, mailing packages, or reserving show tickets. Concierges also work with other departments in the hotel to prepare for large groups, VIP guests, or any guest that may have special needs. Sometimes welcome letters or baskets of fruit are sent to such guests by the concierge desk. However, their duties do not end there. Many hotels provide different levels of concierge service, depending on the type of guest. Penthouse guests can enjoy a private reception, with a separate concierge department to meet their needs, as well as serve them afternoon tea and hot hors d'oeuvres and drinks during the cocktail hour. Some concierge desks also host similar cocktail hours in the lobby.

Sometimes, a request can be more outrageous. Concierges have been known to plan large dinners or receptions on short notice, design entire travel itineraries complete with lodging and tours, rent airplanes or helicopters, secure the front row seats to a sold-out concert or sporting event, or even fill a room with flowers to set the mood for a marriage proposal. Concierges are trained to use their resources and contacts to serve the guest in whatever manner possible. They will, however, refuse to help the guest in any acts unlawful or unkind—no illegal drugs, prostitution, or practical jokes that may be deemed hurtful.

Many of the concierge's duties are performed on their own time, away from the office. They must research any restaurant, tour, attraction, or store before comfortably recommending them to a hotel guest. In addition to visiting the facility, they must verify the price or entrance fee, insurance, and in the case of tours and shuttles, their operator's license. In order to keep current with new museum attractions, concerts, or restaurants, concierges read city magazines and newspapers, as well as hotel trade magazines.

Another important duty of the concierge is to maintain decorum. A good concierge is always well groomed and dressed neatly. They never gossip about the guests. If a guest has a strange request, the concierge should always be very discreet so as not to embarrass the guest or the hotel.

WHAT IS IT LIKE TO BE A CONCIERGE?

Diana Nelson has been a concierge for almost twenty years, her entire career, at the Grand Hyatt Hotel in San Francisco, California, five of which have been as Chief Concierge. A typical day starts at around 8:00 AM when she arrives at the Concierge Desk to put on her name tag and key pin. The crossed gold keys are the symbols of Les Clefs d'Or, the prestigious international association of professional hotel concierges, of which Diana is the current national president.

Because she is the head of the Concierge Desk, Diana must attend morning meetings where she touches base with the hotel manager, group director, and general manager to discuss anticipated groups or other VIPs staying at the hotel. Afterwards she returns to the lobby desk where—along with the three other concierges who assist her—guests' questions, requests, and phone calls are fielded throughout the day, often nonstop.

San Francisco, like other busy cosmopolitan cities, offers endless sights and attractions within the city limits and nearby towns. "To help with time, we have preprinted direction cards for the most popular attractions, such as city sights, the wine country, Fisherman's Wharf," Diana says. Many out-of-town guests ask for restaurant suggestions or the best tours of the city. "We never recommend restaurants, tours, or even shuttles without first visiting the restaurant, taking the tour, or even riding the shuttle bus, and reviewing their contracts and prices. In regard to tours and shuttles, we also have to make sure they have a valid operator's license and are fully insured."

A concierge's job doesn't end once they leave their desk," Diana cautions, "because you are always out in the community making contacts." In their spare time, Diana and the other concierges are often invited to sample tours of the Monterey Peninsula and the wineries in hopes of future recommendations. Restaurants, cafes, and other tourist attractions also do the same. New tour operations try to make the day especially comfortable for Diana and her staff. This definite job perk, according to Diana, is considered "part of concierge-land."

Most requests are for car or limousine rentals, though boats and even helicopters are sometimes in demand. Since many guests also depend on the concierge desk to make travel and flight arrangements for them, it is imperative that a good concierge be familiar with the *Official Airline Guide.* Many business travelers turn to the concierge for help in gathering last-minute secretarial services, office supplies, and computer setups.

Diana admits that while most requests are easily fulfilled, others take a little imagination and sleuthing. "One woman wanted to

To be a successful concierge, you should:

Be very organized and detail-oriented

Have the ability to juggle a number of duties and responsibilities at one time

Be courteous and cheerful with guests and co-workers

Be physically fit since you will spend much of your workday on your feet

Be discreet and respect the privacy of hotel patrons

Be able to handle sometimes hectic and stressful situations

Know the restaurants, tours, museums, and other attractions of the city or area you work in—or be willing to learn them

purchase cookie cutters shaped like the Golden Gate Bridge. After some phone calls, I was able to find a housewares store that sold them." Diana's most important tools are her stable of contacts, most of which are logged into her PC. Modern computers have replaced the clunky Rolodex of the past. It helps a concierge to know where to snag tickets to a sold-out concert or sporting event, or reliable sources to help throw an impromptu cocktail reception.

HAVE I GOT WHAT IT TAKES TO BE A CONCIERGE?

What separates an adequate concierge from a great one? "What you look for in a concierge," Diana offers, "is an attitude. It's the feeling someone has in making a difference in a person's stay and being able to juggle a lot of duties. You almost have to be able to do three or four things at the same time—with a lot of ease."

Diana says organization is key. She keeps her many contacts, from tour operators to food vendors, on computer files. In addition, she keeps a list of fellow Les Clefs d'Or concierges on hand, just in case she needs to call for reinforcements. It is common for concierges to keep information cards on guests that frequent the hotel, noting their particular likes and dislikes, as well as special requests.

//"You almost have to be able to do three or four things at the same time—with a lot of ease."

Knowing the city you work in is important, but as Diana claims, that part can be taught. A concierge spends a considerable amount of time researching restaurants, tours, museums, and other city attractions. How can you recommend a particular boutique without knowing what exactly is sold? Diana and her staff spend their off-hours trying the newest venues in San Francisco, often as guests of the establishment. To keep abreast of current trends, Diana reads *Conde Nast, Travel,* and *Wine Spectator,* as well as the hotel association trades.

Does this sound like a fantasy career so far? Wait—there are downsides to being a concierge. Hard work is not always appreciated. You may have pulled all the stops to plan a wonderful evening complete with dinner, dancing, and drinks atop the most exclusive restaurant in town, as requested by a guest, only to have your suggestions lose to a simple meal served by room service.

Concierges spend much of the day on their feet, greeting guests, making phone calls, running errands, or doing whatever it takes to make things happen. Flexibility is imperative in this job since there is no such thing as "a typical day." A good concierge must be ready to deal with a single guest, or a group of twenty, always in a cheerful and courteous manner. Situations can get hectic, especially when it's the middle of the tourist season, or the hotel is full of conventioneers. Diana turns to her passion for hiking and running to relieve her stress. She admits being an "avid 49ers fan" is the ultimate stress buster.

HOW DO I BECOME A CONCIERGE?

EDUCATION

High School
Diana considers her high school psychology classes helpful to her career, "because you get a little better feel of how people tick." The ability to write well is another skill important to future concierges. Direction cards, hotel communications, and welcome letters to VIP guests are just some examples of where writing counts. Fluency in another language, especially French or Japanese, can be extremely valuable when applying for a job. Interested students should find part-time or seasonal work in order to gain working experience. Your part-time job need not be in a hotel (although that's the best place to make contacts); consider working in the customer service department of a department store. What about working as a junior assistant for a wedding consultant or party caterer? If you are always recruited to show out-of-town relatives the city sights, then at least get paid for your efforts by working for a tour company.

Postsecondary Education
College degrees are not required of all concierges. In fact, many successful and established concierges have a variety of educational and employment backgrounds—from managers to artists to teachers. However, in today's competitive job market it pays to have an edge. Some hotel associations, such as the Educational Institute of the American Hotel and Motel Association offer certification classes for concierges. Only one program, however, is directly involved with the Les Clefs d'Or organization—the International Concierge Institute (ICI). The ICI, in partnership with the International School of Tourism, offers

training and certification courses at their Ft. Lauderdale, Florida or Montreal, Canada, campus. Graduates are given junior Les Clefs d'Or status.

Each eighteen-week program is divided into three modules. The first module, designed to introduce the student to the hospitality industry, has courses on tourism and hotel trends, guest service, and human relations, as well as concierge behavior and protocol. The second module consists of a nine-week internship under the tutelage of a Clefs d'Or member. The last module is an independent study language certification program. The workload of the ICI program is rigorous, and the requirements strict. Many interested students apply for the program, but only a few, those showing potential and aptitude to be a good concierge, are accepted. A degree from the ICI carries its weight—graduates from the ICI are often quickly hired by prestigious hotels around the world.

WHO WILL HIRE ME?

Diana found her job by word of mouth. When Diana entered this career twenty years ago the climate for her profession was very different. "There were not many people doing this (type of job) in the United States," she says. As a manager of a hair salon, she was approached by a salon patron about an opening in the Grand Hyatt's concierge department. "She said I'd be perfect for the job," Diana recalls. She took the woman's tip, and soon found herself working behind the concierge desk with Holly Stiel, the first woman concierge in the United States, as well as the first female to be inducted into the American branch of Les Clefs d'Or.

As chief concierge, Diana is responsible for a staff of fifteen. Newly hired recruits are not allowed to sit at the lobby desk until properly trained. The first few days are spent going over the basic philosophy of being a concierge, and how the hotel expects such an employee to make a difference for the guest. City and tourist attractions come next. "I would put them on a tour. To live in a city and come to that city as a visitor are two totally different things. I like to send them out and see life as a tourist in San Francisco." The fundamentals come next. "You have to teach them how to do the contracts for a car rental, the prices, and the ins and outs of limousines and shuttles."

Many concierge trainees come from other departments of the hotel, such as the front desk. Diana likes to start trainees in the Regency Club, a special service provided by the Grand Hyatt to their VIP guests. Here special guests can relax and are served gourmet food and drinks. The pace is slower, but

WHO WILL HIRE ME?, CONTINUED

expectations high when it comes to service because of the clientele, so it makes a great training ground before concierges are allowed to work the lobby.

As in any career, networking is very important. The Les Clefs d'Or organization runs an informal networking service. The executive secretary, based in Chicago, Illinois, is privy to job openings around the country and keeps a running list of concierge positions available. Any member can discreetly find out about any openings they may be interested in. The ICI also helps place its graduates with concierge positions most suited to the particular candidate.

WHERE CAN I GO FROM HERE?

As in Diana's case, the position of concierge is so interesting and challenging that many keep their jobs their entire working career. However, there are many opportunities for those who want to advance to other departments. Because a concierge's duties are very people-oriented, similar positions, such as a front desk manager, should be considered. If a concierge has a hotel-management or even a business degree, and working experience, as well as superior management skills, they could work for the position of general manager.

Concierges are found in other aspects of business. Besides hotels, concierges are found in some large apartment buildings and condominiums. The concierge services provided at one Chicago high-rise apartment include taking clothes to the cleaners, watering plants, and caring for pets when occupants are out of town. Large upscale department stores such as Nordstrom

In Service Through Friendship: Les Clefs d'Or

The next time you stay at a hotel and need the services of a concierge, pay attention to her lapel. If she is wearing lapel pins of golden crossed keys, then you are in the hands of an experienced concierge. The crossed keys are the symbols of Les Clefs d'Or, the international association of professional hotel concierges. This society was founded in 1929 by Parisian concierge Ferdinand Gillet to serve as a support system for concierges working in Europe. The organization grew and became international in 1970—today there are thirty participating national sections with a membership over four thousand strong. The U.S. Les Clefs d'Or is headed by Diana Nelson, chief concierge at the Grand Hyatt Hotel in San Francisco, California.

Membership requirements are high—in addition to having at least five years of experience, candidates must be sponsored by a current Clefs d'Or member, obtain a written recommendation by their hotel general manager, and pass an examination. The goal of Les Clefs d'Or is to maintain a standard of guest service quality. Members are given training opportunities in order to hone their concierge skills and techniques when dealing with the public. The membership roster is a valuable tool for support, or help from fellow concierges when faced with a difficult request. This support system is true to the Clefs d'Or motto "In service through friendship."

offer concierge service for its shoppers, from complimentary coat and package checking to restaurant and store information. Nordstrom concierges also offer tours of the store.

The extremely ambitious can also consider starting their own concierge business. Personal concierges strive to be personal assistants to those too busy to organize their home or run errands. For a fixed price, personal concierges are responsible for a set of weekly duties; special requests, such as planning dinner parties or buying Christmas gifts, are charged extra. Since retainer fees for a personal concierge are steep—anywhere from $400 to $600 a month—people requiring such services are either extremely busy, very wealthy, or both.

WHAT ARE SOME RELATED JOBS?

Because of the uniqueness of this career, the U.S. Department of Labor does not yet classify the career of concierge. Similar workers are people responsible for guest service. *Bell captains,* since they are often stationed prominently near the front of the lobby, are often asked directions to city attractions or for suggestions on where to go. Hotel guests can also turn to any front desk worker for basic questions or help and receive satisfactory information. Elaborate requests are another matter, however. The concierge's position, because of the commitment to guest service and attention to detail, is unique. There really is no other department quite like it.

Some other service-related careers that are similar to concierges include tour guides, travel agents, camp directors, caterers, cruise directors, party planners, personal assistants, and wedding consultants.

Related Jobs

Bell captains

Camp directors

Caterers

Cruise directors

Party planners

Personal assistants

Tour guides

Travel agents

Wedding consultants

WHAT ARE THE SALARY RANGES?

According to the ICI, expect to earn in the low- to mid-twenties as a new concierge. An experienced concierge, with Les Clefs d'Or status, working at a large urban hotel, can expect to earn around $50,000 a year. The usual benefits include paid vacations, sick and holiday time, health insurance, and some type of employee hotel discount, depending on the establishment.

A concierge, especially a good one, is often given tips or gifts by grateful hotel patrons. Nancy Girard, ICI's director of communications, says concierge service is one provided by the hotel, and is absolutely free to any guest. "The little things like making reservations or giving directions are easy for a concierge to do. But if the concierge can do something great to make a visit memorable, then the guest may want to thank them in a special way."

Nancy recalls one concierge who was asked by a wealthy traveler to come up with a very unusual birthday gift for his son on short notice. After some maneuvering the concierge was able to meet the demand—a souped-up army tank—and had it shipped overseas in time for the birthday. Needless to say, the concierge was tipped well for his effort. Concierges, ethically, cannot and will not press for tips. The hotel guest decides whether to tip, and, if so, how much.

WHAT IS THE JOB OUTLOOK?

Job opportunities look bright for those interested in a concierge career. A healthy economy allows for more travel, for both business and personal reasons. Look for jobs in large urban cities of New York, Los Angeles, and Chicago; tourist-heavy areas such as California and Florida, and the convention mecca of Las Vegas. Employment opportunities are plentiful abroad, although European standards and training may be different from those found in the United States (check with the ICI). For those eager for challenges outside of the hotel industry, try cruise lines, rental properties, or consider setting up your own concierge business.

Busier lifestyles leave little time for mundane chores or last-minute details. Many travelers, once shy or intimidated by the concierge desk, realize this is a free service available for their convenience. As people travel more frequently, they become more savvy. At a hundred to almost two hundred dollars a night for a double room, guests expect more than a bed and cable television. They are paying for a sense of luxury. Hotel general managers realize that a concierge department can provide the ultimate in guest services; and it is that type of service that makes a hotel a true luxury hotel. Even many smaller hotels, especially those that cater to business travelers, are now providing concierge service.

Some hotels have experimented with computerized kiosks that display tour and restaurant information. Though kiosks may cost less compared to maintaining a concierge department, it does not provide one-to-one personalized service hotel guests desire. Also, kiosks cannot make a true recommenda-tion since tour operators and restaurants pay a service fee to be advertised in the kiosk listing.

There are many stories about the crazy and fantastic requests concierges are asked to fulfill. Concierges who are able to meet the challenge are certainly imaginative and resourceful. However, it is not completing the near impossible that makes a concierge; rather it is performing well the simple requests for car rentals or directions to the city museums that make a good concierge—one people trust and identify with true guest service.

Hotel Desk Clerk

SUMMARY

DEFINITION
Desk clerks *work the front desk and are responsible for performing a variety of services for the hotel guests such as registration, room assignments, and providing general information.*

ALTERNATIVE JOB TITLES
Front office clerk
Reservation clerk
Room clerk

SALARY REQUIREMENTS
$8,800 to $24,000 to $30,000

EDUCATIONAL REQUIREMENTS
High school degree or equivalent

CERTIFICATION OR LICENSING
None

EMPLOYMENT OUTLOOK
Faster than the average

HIGH SCHOOL SUBJECTS
Business
Computers
Mathematics
Psychology

PERSONAL INTERESTS
Computers
Helping people: personal service

Lynda Witry swiped the credit card a third time. Another denial flashed on the terminal. "I'm very sorry, Mr. Jones, your credit card was denied for some reason," she said quietly so the other guests in line would not hear. "Do you want to try a different card?" As Mr. Jones chose another card from his wallet, Lynda could see the lines getting longer, and the guests becoming more impatient.

Numerous lines on the PBX were ringing, so Lynda answered a call while she ran Mr. Jones' second credit card through the register. "As a matter of fact, the checkout lines are extremely long right now," she reported to a hotel guest. "I suggest you try the video checkout system found on Channel 15 of your television. It's very user friendly, and your folio will be mailed directly to your home address."

Mr. Jones' credit is finally approved. Lynda quickly completes the check-out process and hands a flustered Mr. Jones his folio. "Thank you for being so patient. We hope to see you again at the Giorgios Hotel," she says with a smile.

Lynda turns to the next guest in line. "Hello. Welcome to the Giorgios Hotel. How can I help you?"

WHAT DOES A DESK CLERK DO?

The functions of the *front office worker,* also known as the *desk clerk,* can be separated into four categories: process reservations, register the guest, serve as primary guest liaison, and process guest departure.

Process reservations. The desk clerk, or more specifically, the *reservation clerk,* handles the duties of guest reservations, most often over the phone. They determine if the requested date is available, quote rates, record advance deposits or prepayments, confirm room reservation, and describe policies and services to the guest. Reservation clerks, when dealing with reservation discrepancies, may have to retrieve hotel records, or change or cancel the reservation in order to resolve the problem to the guest's satisfaction. Reservation clerks must also analyze the guest's special needs while at the hotel, and relay them to the proper department.

Register the guest. After greeting the guest, desk clerks obtain and verify the required registration information such as the guest's name, address, and length of stay. A credit card is usually required as a deposit or guarantee. Once the paperwork is done, room keys or key cards are issued, and guests are directed to their rooms.

Primary guest liaison. Desk clerks often act as a buffer between the hotel and the guest. When guests have problems, have special requests, or encounter difficulties, they usually turn to the most visible person for help—the desk clerk. Some services provided to guests are laundry and valet requests, wake-up calls, and delivery of mail or messages. Clerks may also provide general information regarding the hotel or surrounding community. Their most important task, however, is to quickly address requests and complaints, or redirect the guest to the proper department.

Process guest departure. In some lodging establishments, if desired, a guest can choose to settle his or her account while in the room via the express, or video, checkout. Room charges are tallied on screen and charged to the customer's credit card. Video checkouts are settled by desk clerks at the end of the day, and folios sent to the guest's home address. However, many people still choose to personally check out at the front desk. After verifying and explaining all room charges, the desk clerk can begin to settle the guest's account. Sometimes, if credit authorization is declined, they may have to politely negotiate an alternate method of payment. After thanking the guest and

Lingo to Learn

Cash out: Before closing a shift, desks must balance cash, checks, and credit card slips with the amount of business done for that particular shift.

Folio: A hotel bill listing all room charges, including long-distance phone calls, food and beverage service, and cable.

PBX: Private Branch Exchange; a hotel's private telephone switchboard.

RevPar: The amount of money the hotel earns per month.

New Technology

New computer programs are constantly being developed to make the check-in process easier and faster. The Mobile Zip-In program, developed and created by Geoteck Communications, Inc., for the Hilton Hotel Corporation, allows guests to check into their room while riding in the hotel's shuttle bus. The guest must swipe a frequent guest hotel card, or major credit card, through a mobile data unit, and the information is immediately relayed to the front desk. The guest is presented with his or her key card as soon as the bus reaches the hotel's front doors.

listening to any comments, positive or negative, the desk clerk can move on to the next customer or task.

Front office workers are responsible for keeping the hotel's information systems up to date. Many hotels are now keeping detailed information on their guests—such as the reason for their stay, their likes and dislikes—and use this information for future marketing needs. Depending on the type or size of the hotel, they may also be responsible for working the switchboard, bookkeeping, house banks and petty cash, daily bank deposits, and recording key cards. In addition, they must keep the front desk area clean and presentable.

WHAT IS IT LIKE TO BE A DESK CLERK?

Lynda Witry started her career in the hotel industry three years ago as a front desk clerk. She is currently the day front desk supervisor for the Giorgios Hotel and Conference Center (a division of Comfort Inn), in Orland Park, Illinois. Lynda is also finishing up her senior year in hotel management at Purdue University.

The day shift begins at 7:00 AM. The Giorgios Hotel caters to the business traveler and many conferences or seminars are held at the facility. One of Lynda's first responsibilities of the day is to check out any meeting space that is to be used. Requested office supplies, such as notepads, pencils, pens, or audiovisual equipment, must be set up before the room is opened. If food and beverage service is ordered, that too must be set up.

The hotel's check out time is noon, but many business travelers, anxious to catch their flight or get to their next meeting, check out earlier. Lynda must process each room quickly, but accurately, so checkout lines don't get too long. Room charges, along with any cable or room service fees, are tallied, explained, and verified with the guest. The front desk can get very busy from 10 AM until past noon.

When the desk quiets down, Lynda takes care of her other duties. "We have to check on availability so the hotel is not overbooked or sold out. We also have to process meeting charges, and make sure any food is charged to the room." Lynda also needs to prepare for the next wave of guests. "We have to check our arrivals list, and make sure there are registration cards for every person arriving. Answering phones and making new reservations can keep you pretty busy. The afternoon is quiet until about 2:00 PM, depending on the number of check-ins and how early everyone wants to get in." At the end of the shift, Lynda cashes out and balances all credit card receipts and cash.

> **// Answering phones and making new reservations can keep you pretty busy."**

The front desk is open twenty-four hours a day. Lynda's morning shift is 7:00 AM to 3:00 PM; the afternoon shift is from 3:00 to 11:00 PM. The midnight shift is taken by the *night audit person,* whose main duty is to enter the day's room charges into the computer. Business people usually travel during the first part of the week, Monday through Thursday; convention or group travelers are more common from Thursday to Saturday.

Since the hotel has adjoining banquet facilities, wedding parties often reserve blocks of rooms. Needless to say, many wedding guests are still in a party mood long after the reception ends. Lynda recalls having to ask noisy guests to tone down and warn them of the hotel's policies. "Usually a phone call is enough. Sometimes, I've had to go up to the room and speak to them directly. If I have to warn them a third time, that's it—they're out." In such cases, Lynda calls security to escort the offending guests out of the hotel—with no refunds.

HAVE I GOT WHAT IT TAKES TO BE A DESK CLERK?

As with any front-of-the-house department, the front desk often serves as the guest's first impression of the hotel. "Desk clerks should be great communicators," says Lynda. "They need to be able to deal with different kinds of people to be successful in this job." Desk clerks should be courteous and eager to help, even at times when the guests are demanding. On occasions when guests have questions or requests that the front desk can't meet, the front desk must be able to relay the demands to the proper department.

To be a successful desk clerk or front office worker, you should:

Have neat handwriting

Be courteous and level-headed, especially when dealing with difficult guests

Relay information accurately and efficiently

Be flexible to handle many different tasks at the same time

Be well groomed and dressed conservatively

Be physically fit since you will be on your feet most of your workday

They must be organized, flexible, and patient since they often need to handle many different situations and tasks simultaneously. Reservations for large groups can be complicated and time consuming, especially when there are other guests waiting in line.

Since they spend the majority of the day on their feet, desk clerks should be in good physical condition.

Successful desk clerks are comfortable working with computers and are not afraid to learn new programs. A clear speaking voice is essential, especially when taking reservations over the phone. Good penmanship is another desirable quality. Fluency in other languages, though not a requirement, is a great plus.

Good grooming habits are essential for the job. Many hotels enforce a strong professional dress code since front desk workers have high visibility. Hair should be neatly pulled back—no "big hair" allowed. Men's hair should be cut short in back and over the ears. Excessive jewelry is frowned upon, as is heavy or dramatic makeup. Desk clerks wear uniforms provided by the hotel. Some hotels also provide dry cleaning free of charge.

Since hotels are open twenty-four hours a day, it may be necessary for new employees with little seniority to work less-desirable shifts. Some holiday work should be expected.

HOW DO I BECOME A DESK CLERK?

EDUCATION

High School

High school classes can be a useful foundation for a career in the hotel industry. Concentrate on classes such as human relations, business or marketing, and even sociology to prepare yourself for this people-oriented job. Lynda found her high school computer classes helpful, as well as the typing classes. "Being able to type—not the hunt-and-peck method—makes working on the computer faster." According to Lynda, it helps to know how to compute percentages and discounts, so don't forget your math!

Postsecondary Training

If you are hoping to use a desk clerk job as a stepping stone for management, you should seriously consider a degree in hotel management. Though advancement is still possible without a college degree, it may take much longer. Promotions may even be passed to employees with equal work experience, but who are better educated. There are hundreds of colleges and universities that offer two- or four-year programs. Check with your high school career center for a listing, or contact the Educational Institute of the American Hotel and Motel Association.

College courses that help Lynda in her job are Human Relations, Finance, and practical classes such as Hospitality Supervision and Front Office Procedures.

INTERNSHIPS

Internships are a great way to earn work experience, course credit, and most importantly, a chance to distinguish yourself from other applicants come interview time. Lynda fondly recalls her internship as hospitality hostess with one of the five-hundred-bed theme resorts at Walt Disney World in Orlando, Florida. "I found the internship through a school job seminar. They (Disney World) had recruiters doing fifteen-minute interviews on site. You were notified the next day if you were hired or not." Though her position gave her limited responsibility, having a Disney internship on her resume is very impressive.

WHO WILL HIRE ME?

Desk clerks are needed at every hotel and motel. The amount of responsibilities given depend on the size and type of lodging establishment. Larger hotels may have separate departments, each responsible for answering phones, making advance reservations, or processing guest arrivals. The pace of work may be more frenzied at times because of the higher guest count. Smaller hotels, on the other hand, may have to combine departments to accommodate a smaller staff.

Beth Coen, a front desk manager for the Holiday Inn-Crown Plaza in Indianapolis, Indiana, prefers working for a smaller hotel. "There is more responsibility given to employees at smaller properties, plus a higher level of camaraderie among the workers." Many of her front office staff have been loyal long-term employees of the hotel.

This industry, as a rule, tends to have a high turnover rate. Larger hotels, especially those located in busy urban areas, may offer faster opportunities for advancement. Job openings are created as people climb up the corporate ladder or leave the workforce for other reasons.

Beth found her first job in the hotel industry by answering a classified ad in the paper. Look under the headings "Hotel," "Motel," "Office Worker," or "Hospitality." Many jobs are posted in trade magazines such as *Lodging* and *Hosteur,* or in hotel employee newsletters. Don't forget the importance of networking—let your teachers know you are serious about a future hospitality career. They may have important contacts or information to help your job search; or they may be privy to job openings in the field. High school job centers and their counselors are helpful in providing guidance to interested students like yourself. Career centers have occupational handbooks, trade magazines, and literature on college or vocational programs. They may even post part-time or seasonal work available in the field.

Hiring requirements vary from employer to employer, but most hotels look for candidates with work experience as well as education. Many desk clerks have a high school degree or the equivalent; but those ambitious to someday run the management track should consider obtaining an associate's or bachelor's degree in hotel management, or a similar program. When applying for a job, experience in the hotel industry is a definite plus. However, experience in the restaurant trade, customer service, or retail is also valuable.

Beth says she would consider hiring people straight from high school if they were responsible, professional, and very ambitious.

Advancement possibilities

Front office managers *supervise all front office personnel such as reservation and desk clerks, secretaries, concierges, bellhops, valets, and doormen.*

General managers *are responsible for every aspect of the hotel and its operation. They direct other members of the management team, interact with and evaluate employees, approve expenditures, set room rates, and establish standards for hotel decor, beverage and food service, and all guest services.*

WHERE CAN I GO FROM HERE?

Once she earns her degree in hotel management, Lynda hopes to explore other departments within the hospitality industry. "I am really interested in the training and development aspect of the business—maybe even human resources."

Desk clerks and reservation clerks are both considered entry-level positions. Promotions within the front office could lead to jobs as front desk supervisor or front office manager. Further advancement may be as assistant hotel manager. It is also possible to move on to other departments within the hotel, such as banquets, or the sales department. Job promotions, especially to the management level, will be easier to obtain with further education.

Most of the skills needed to be a good desk clerk are learned on the job. On-site training is the only practical method since many of the computer programs used by the front office are hotel-specific, varying from property to property. The way desk clerks handle guests depends on the hotel's preferences. Other hotels may choose to send their employees, especially those destined for management, to off-site seminars or further education classes. This highly monitored method of training will continue in the future. Lynda agrees, "It's the best way to learn."

WHAT ARE SOME RELATED JOBS?

The U.S. Department of Labor classifies desk clerks under the heading, Administrative Support Occupation. Also under this heading are people who work the reservation desk, called *reservation clerks.* In addition to processing advance reservations over the phone or by mail, they are responsible for monitoring guest room availability so the hotel is never oversold. *Mail and information clerks,* usually found in very large hotels, distribute guests' mail, faxes, and packages. Night audit clerks, also called *night room clerks,* work the midnight shift and are responsible for some bookkeeping or cashiering duties. Since they usually work with little or no staff support, they also serve as the hotel's *night general managers.*

Other careers that offer duties similar to that of hotel desk clerks include bank tellers, airline travel and ticket agents, counter and retail clerks, dispatchers, interviewing and new account clerks, lobby attendants, security guards, museum guides and ushers, receptionists, record clerks, survey workers, and telephone operators.

Related Jobs

Airline travel and ticket agents

Bank tellers

Counter and retail clerks

Dispatchers

Interviewing and new account clerks

Lobby attendants

Mail and information clerks

Museum guides and ushers

Night audit clerks

Night general manager

Receptionists

Record clerks

Security guards

Survey workers

Telephone operators

WHAT ARE THE SALARY RANGES?

Desk clerks are paid hourly. Lynda says there is a difference in entry-level pay between urban and suburban hotels. "Suburban hotels pay about $6 to $7 an hour. Larger urban hotels can pay $9 to $10 an hour. Most clerks would probably top out at $8 to $10 an hour."

A recent salary survey conducted by the American Hotel & Motel Association shows a difference according to the size and the type of hotel—economy, suites, or first class. The average front office clerk earns about $6 an hour at an economy hotel; $6.80 an hour at a suite hotel; and $7 an hour at a first-class property. However, this same survey shows that suite hotels award a higher year-end bonus for front office workers, an average of about $1,600 compared to an $180 average bonus at a first class hotel.

After a probationary period, usually ninety days, the front office worker is frequently offered medical and sometimes dental insurance, vacation and sick days, paid holidays, and employee discounts.

WHAT IS THE JOB OUTLOOK?

The future of this career is bright. As long as the economy is healthy, people will continue to travel, whether for business or pleasure. Hotels that have facilities for seminars and conferences will stay busy. Families today prefer to take short, but frequent trips, as opposed to week-long vacations. All these factors validate the need for dependable desk clerks to work the front desk, and reservation clerks to sell the rooms.

Jobs will be most plentiful with hotels located in busy urban areas, where there tend to be higher turnover rates. Larger hotels are known to pay higher wages, promote faster, and may be more open to sending employees to further education classes and seminars. Any downsides to working in the big city? The higher cost of living will probably eat up the pay difference. Also, employees of large-staffed hotels tend to experience less camaraderie among co-workers.

Software programs are a great help to the front office. For example, the Front Desk Resort Management System (RMS) outdates the master registry book by keeping track of reservations and guest information. Many guests now opt to use the in-room video express checkout instead of waiting in line. Even with such technological advancements desk clerks are still needed to head the front desk. Guests still like personal attention to certain details, such as answering their questions and handling special requests. Even video checkouts must be processed by desk clerks, and folios mailed to guests.

Even though this is an entry-level position, it is an important one. For many guests, the front office worker gives them their first impression of the hotel. Desk clerks who are personable, driven, and hardworking, as well as educated and trained, will succeed in this field.

Hotel Executive Housekeeper

SUMMARY

DEFINITION
Hotel executive housekeepers direct and control the staff and operations of housekeeping departments within the hotel.

ALTERNATIVE JOB TITLES
Director of housekeeping
Director of housekeeping services
Housekeeping administrator
Housekeeping coordinator
Housekeeping manager

SALARY RANGE
$20,591 to $36,974 to $110,000

EDUCATIONAL REQUIREMENTS
High school diploma; Associate's or bachelor's degree for managerial positions

CERTIFICATION OR LICENSING
Recommended

EMPLOYMENT OUTLOOK
Faster than the average

HIGH SCHOOL SUBJECTS
Business
English (writing/literature)
Mathematics
Psychology
Sociology
Speech

PERSONAL INTERESTS
Business management
Helping people: emotionally
Helping people: personal service
Teaching

Jackie Martin can probably find her way around the hotel blindfolded. As director of housekeeping, she participates in a daily walk-around with the hotel's general manager. Touring the property keeps Jackie and her housekeeping staff on their toes.

"The lobby areas are perfect," Jackie thinks to herself as they pass tables of gleaming brass and dark wood furniture arranged just so. The public cleaning crew is setting up their automatic polishers to tackle the marble floors. It has just started to rain outside, but the cleaning crews and bell team are on top of things and quickly spread out floor mats to keep lobby floors dry and safe. The general manager nods approvingly.

On their way up to the seventh floor, the general manager comments on the cleanliness of the elevator area. "Thanks," Jackie replies. "The new glass cleaner we purchased is working well, it's ammonia-free, plus it has a shorter dwell time. My cleaning crews really work hard, and I must say I'm proud of them."

The last stop on the walk-around is the pool and health club. As soon as they enter the ladies' changing area, Jackie senses trouble. The counters are wet and cluttered with towels; the mirrors streaked. There are more wet towels hung over dressing room doors and benches. A stray swimming cap peaks out from under a chair. "I'll make sure the attendants get to this right away!" Jackie offers as the general manager's eyebrows rise.

Tomorrow's main pre-shift meeting topic: Better maintenance of the health spa.

WHAT DOES AN EXECUTIVE HOUSEKEEPER DO?

Housekeeping departments can be found in many institutions—hospitals, businesses, colleges and universities, and condominiums, among others. They are especially important in the hotel and motel industry. Imagine what a five hundred-bed hotel would look like without the housekeeping staff. Linens would remain unchanged, hallways cluttered, ashtray receptacles full, packets of glycerin soap nonexistent, and the toilet paper wouldn't have the fancy three-point fold. HELP!

A large part of any hotel's reputation rests on its appearance. A posh hotel would lose some of its grandeur if the lobby looked cluttered and dirty. Hotel patrons don't mind paying higher room fees because they are guaranteed some measure of luxury, if only for a night or two. Since all guests—whether paying $19.99 at the Motel 6, or $200 a night at the Hotel Intercontinental—expect their rooms to be neat and orderly, the housekeeping staff is vital to the success of any motel or hotel. At the helm of the housekeeping department is the executive housekeeper, or the director of housekeeping services. The primary duty of the executive housekeeper is to ensure the cleanliness of the hotel. In order to achieve

Lingo to Learn

Break the house: *Give room or floor assignments to attendants and public cleaners.*

Cart: *A wheeled pushcart used by room attendants to hold their supplies of linens, towel, soaps, and toiletries, as well as cleaning solutions and cleaning instruments.*

Cleaning friendly: *Furniture or materials that can be cleaned easily, with little damage or wear and tear.*

Dwell time: *The maximum number of minutes it takes for cleaning solutions to do their job. Example: Bathroom cleaning solutions need a dwell time of nine minutes to dissolve soap scum before it can be rinsed or wiped off. Waiting more or less than that optimum time will cause the solution to lose its potency.*

Line level: *Entry-level employee with little formal education or training.*

Property: *The hotel and its exterior grounds.*

Walk-around: *Inspection of different areas of the hotel, usually done by the executive housekeeper and general manager.*

this, they must supervise, coordinate, and direct the activities of the hotel housekeeping department. The executive housekeeper determines the cleaning needs of different areas in the hotel lobby, sleeping rooms, restaurants, pools—and schedules cleaning crews accordingly. Areas are inspected regularly to make certain safety standards and departmental policies are being met. He or she hires and trains the cleaning staff, as well as recommends promotions, transfers, and if necessary, dismissals. Executive housekeepers are also responsible for keeping inventory of cleaning supplies and equipment, as well as hotel linens, towels, and soaps. They deal directly with vendors to learn of the latest in cleaning solutions, equipment, and techniques.

The cleaning of uniforms worn by the hotel staff and all hotel laundry are the executive housekeeper's responsibility as well. He or she prepares reports concerning room occupancy, department budget expenses, and employees' work records for payroll. Some executive housekeepers may help in decorating the hotel. Some also direct the setup for conventions and banquets.

Though executive housekeepers may share in some of the cleaning duties, in larger hotels their role is mostly administrative. Some extremely busy hotels may even hire *assistant executive housekeepers* or *assistant directors* to share in the administrative duties of keeping house. Supervisors and shift supervisors are directly responsible for the employees and the work done on their particular shift. (Hotels run twenty-four hours a day, so many have implemented a three-shift system.) *Floor managers* and *inspectors* supervise the team of room attendants assigned to a particular floor. A *status person* handles any special requests a guest might make while at the hotel.

The cleaning staff works hard to keep the lobby neat and orderly. They empty trash cans and ashtrays, gather glasses from the lobby tables, dust furniture, clean mirrors, and vacuum carpets and rugs. Hotel restaurants are also cleaned and maintained throughout the day. Pools and health clubs must be cleaned and sanitized. *Room attendants* are responsible for the guest rooms. They tidy sleeping rooms and bathrooms, replenish towels, soaps, shampoos, and lotions, as well as attend to any special requests for cribs, ironing boards, or extra supplies. They also stock and keep records of the mini-bar.

WHAT IS IT LIKE TO BE AN EXECUTIVE HOUSEKEEPER?

7:00 AM: Jackie Martin, director of housekeeping for the Sheraton Hotel and Towers in Chicago, begins her ten-hour day by reviewing the previous day's house count. "I get together with the other managers to break out the house."

This involves giving floor and room assignments to floor managers and room attendants for the day. "We hand out rooms for all the ladies, and make sure everything is covered."

Jackie tries to touch base with all her workers. One way to do this is by holding short meetings with every shift. "We have a pre-shift meeting with everybody, about ten to fifteen minutes, about the different groups in house (staying at the hotel) and what their special requirements are. We discuss different topics of the day."

Once the room attendants and their floor managers begin their assignments, Jackie heads up to the hotel's executive offices for more meetings. "I meet with the director of reception, the hotel manager, and the general manager for a quick fifteen-minute meeting about what's going on in the hotel for the day, and any challenges we may face." The previous day's house count, special hotel groups, and other issues and any problems are also discussed. Like all housekeeping professionals, Jackie is a good communicator. It's important to be able to meet with hotel executives as well as line-level employees on a daily basis.

Every day, Jackie tours the hotel for inspection. "We do a walk-around with the general manager. You don't see that at every property, but we make a point to do so at the Sheraton." Walk-arounds are done to make sure areas of the hotel are clean, orderly, and up to the cleaning and safety standards of the hotel. Areas of the hotel that don't measure up are noted and fixed for the next walk-around. "It's tough, but a really great thing to do, because then you are always on top of your property."

The rest of the day is spent planning for special events and conferences, and future house counts. In-house counts are important to the hotel in general, and the housekeeping department in particular. If a heavier-than-normal guest load is expected, or if special guests, or large conventions are expected, then Jackie can plan ahead. In order to accommodate a full house, extra room attendants, cleaners, and floor managers are needed, as well as more supplies. Vendors promote the latest cleaning solution, machinery, or technique needed to make hotel cleanup easier and faster. Other supplies, from bathroom fixtures to wrinkle-free sheets, are also ordered from different vendors. A large part of the executive housekeeper's job is to research, sample, and eventually order supplies for the hotel. Larger hotels, such as the Sheraton, have product managers who are responsible for this duty.

From time to time, special projects arise that need the attention of the executive housekeeper. Currently, Jackie is taking part in the renovation project of the Sheraton. She is meeting with designers heading the renovation work to make sure their designs and furniture are workable. "My concerns have a cleaning angle. Are the materials chosen cleaning friendly? Are the patterns good?"

Jackie's input probably saved the housekeeping department future headaches. "I had some definite concerns with some of the designs. Luckily, they are tweaking some of their materials for heavier fabrics and woods."

HAVE I GOT WHAT IT TAKES TO BE AN EH?

WANTED: A hardworking individual who doesn't faint at the thought of hundreds, maybe thousands of dirty toilets, wet towels, and butt-filled ashtrays. Must be a great communicator and able to deal with many types of people—from highly educated to line-level. Self-motivation a plus. The squeamish or those who thrive on gratitude need not apply.

Still interested in becoming an executive housekeeper? It takes a lot to succeed in this field. Because the position of executive housekeeper is the top rung of the department ladder, you should be prepared to work hard in order to make the climb.

Room attendants, the basic entry-level position, have a heavy and strenuous workload. Their assigned rooms must be cleaned not only during their shift, but also before new guests can check into the hotel, usually by early afternoon. They push heavy carts containing fresh linens, towels, and supplies. Much of the cleaning calls for bending and lifting, so attendants must be in good physical condition. According to Kay Wireck, executive housekeeper for Bally's Casino and Resort, a 2,833-room hotel in Las Vegas, "Room attendants are responsible for about 15 rooms daily, during a 7-hour shift (1 hour is considered lunch and break time). That's a lot of work. If it is an occupied room, they spend about 15 to 20 minutes straightening up; if it is a check-out room, attendants spend considerable time cleaning the room for the next guest, about 30 minutes or more."

Executive housekeepers and assistant housekeeping directors, shift supervisors, and inspectors need to be good communicators to keep their staff happy and working well. These supervisors are directly responsible for their assigned areas, and any problems or complaints that occur must be addressed immediately. Motivation is key when working with large cleaning staffs. If in a pinch, good managers help with cleaning duties. "It helps to know what is expected from all employees, at whatever level, firsthand. It gives you credibility, and respect from your staff," Kay maintains.

The hours are long and stressful. Many executive housekeepers work ten or more hours a day in order to touch base with all three work shifts. Some weekend and holiday work can be expected, depending on the business demands.

To be a successful executive housekeeper, you should:

Be organized

Be able to solve problems, as well as foresee and address future ones

Be a good communicator who is able to work with co-workers and guests

Have flexibility in regard to duties and responsibilities

Be a hard worker and willing to work long hours

For Kay, the most rewarding part of her job is working with people. "It pleases me to help employees achieve goals in their career, and observe them going up the ladder to higher positions." As with most service-oriented jobs, customers' complaints are inevitable. "Some complaints are credible," says Kay. "Others are not." It is the manager's job to assess the situation and resolve the problem.

HOW DO I BECOME AN EXECUTIVE HOUSEKEEPER?

EDUCATION

High School
If you are interested in pursuing a career as a housekeeping executive, start in high school. Business subjects, general science, and chemistry classes serve as a solid educational foundation. Speech and English courses will boost your communication skills.

Match your education with experience. Summer and holiday breaks are great times to work in the field. Jackie says that the Sheraton Hotel regularly hires high school students for summer work in the laundry department. If part-time work at a hotel near you is not available, try getting a cleaning job at a local hospital, business, or school. No matter where you find student employment, it's important to get a feel for institutional work. You should look in the classified section of the paper, church bulletins, and your school guidance office for job leads.

Postsecondary Training
Some smaller hotels and motels will hire candidates based on their amount of experience. However, with today's competitive market, it is increasingly important to have further education. A bachelor's degree in hotel management from

an accredited school is your best bet, but associate's degrees are valued as well. Interested students like yourself should emphasize course work in business administration, accounting, budgeting, and economics. Don't forget communication, sociology, and psychology—you'll need it when dealing with a large, diverse staff. Other useful classes are interior design and purchasing.

As always, pay your dues now. Apply for part-time or seasonal housekeeping work—or perhaps a hotel internship—and put your skills to the test. Such jobs are more impressive on a resume than working at the local mall. In fact, many recruiters pay more attention to former interns than to those with no past affiliation to the hotel.

Even after landing your first housekeeping position, you should still consider taking continuing education classes to keep current with the industry. Thorough knowledge of often-changing labor laws and safety regulations, sanitation laws, and maintenance and control are keys to your success. Basic computer knowledge would also be helpful.

INTERNSHIPS

Internships can give you a taste of the career without the pressures and obligations of a full-time job. The experience can also bridge your academic history with actual work experience. This will look very impressive on your resume.

The best source of information about such opportunities are professional organizations and trade magazines. Get the latest issue of *Executive Housekeeping Today* for good leads. This particular magazine is published by the National Executive Housekeepers Association, an organization of over eight thousand professionals in the housekeeping field, which, in addition to providing continuing education, certificate, and collegiate degree programs, also maintains a referral service.

Your school career center will have helpful information on internships available, as well as career books, magazines, and counselors to guide you. Don't forget to ask your teachers if they know of job opportunities before the center does. Post your resume on America Online's Career Center, or research the countless internships and scholarships that are posted by schools, hotels, and motels across the world. Be sure to check out our "Surf the Web" chapter near the end of this book, too.

CERTIFICATION OR LICENSING

Certification or registration is not required of executive housekeepers, though it is something many seek. It is often considered a measure of professional success. The International Executive Housekeepers Association, among other institutions, offers two designations—Certified Executive Housekeeper (CEH), or Registered Executive Housekeeper (REH). Qualified individuals earn a CEH by fulfilling educational requirements through a certificate program, a self-study program, or a college degree program.

REH, the highest designation offered by the International Executive Housekeepers Association, can be earned by completing a collegiate program. The REH program calls for a 360-hour program, while the CEH requires 320 hours. Both programs are divided into two areas—management skills, and technical and administration skills. Among the courses are Staffing and Staff Development, Management Philosophy, Housekeeping Techniques, and Laundry and Linen.

WHO WILL HIRE ME?

Jackie stresses that all avenues should be tried when looking for a job in this field. "Get in touch with all your contacts," she advises. One of her first hotel jobs was as a *furniture and fixtures expert.* Jackie was in charge of renovation work, from designing new color schemes to buying new furniture and the right accessories for different hotels. She worked as a floor manager for other smaller Sheraton hotels before landing this position at the Sheraton Hotel and Towers.

Sunday job sections are great places for leads. Look under "Hotel," "Motel," "Housekeeping," or "Hospitality" for companies currently hiring. Trade magazines have sections where job opportunities are posted. The Educational Institute of the American Hotel and Motel Association maintains a Web site for job openings around the country as well as a site to post your resume. You can also meet recruiters face to face at job fairs—have your resume ready to circulate. First impres-

What does it take to run the Sheraton's housekeeping department every week?

You'd be surprised at the number of workers and supplies needed to keep up the Sheraton Hotel and Towers in downtown Chicago. Here are some of the stats:

It takes over 100 room attendants and 32 public cleaners to clean this 1,204-bed hotel.

85,785 towels are used weekly.

Bedsheets are changed daily, which adds up to 64,533 pieces of linen a week.

1,806 bedspreads are used every week.

98,000 pounds of laundry are washed in house. Call Maytag!

8,100 rolls of toilet paper and 8,500 packets of soap are supplied in all guest rooms.

Over 200 gallons of various cleaning solutions are used to keep the hotel sparkling.

About 6,300 cans of soda are purchased from the mini-bar.

sions are important too, so make sure you look the part of the hotel professional.

If you want a more hands-on type of job, consider working for smaller motels or hotels, especially those away from metropolitan areas. Those establishments are guaranteed to have a small housekeeping department—the smaller the staff, the more likely the executive housekeeper shares in cleaning duties. Jobs are more plentiful, however, in busy urban areas where larger hotels and motels are needed. Bigger hotels mean more rooms and areas to clean, which warrants a larger cleaning staff. Pay attention to tourist-heavy areas like Las Vegas and Florida, where new hotels and resorts are being built to accommodate the demand.

> **//Start early and gather valuable experience working as summer help at a hotel. Education is important, as is good experience."**

Jackie's advice for future executive housekeepers? "Start early and gather valuable experience working as summer help at a hotel. Education is important, as is good experience." However, she notes that a college degree is key to advancement. "It depends on what you want out of your career. If you desire a managerial position, a college background will get you there quicker."

WHERE CAN I GO FROM HERE?

Don't expect to graduate and immediately land a corner office with a name plate that reads "Director of Housekeeping." "Most college graduates start out as floor managers or supervisors," notes Jackie. "They need to work themselves up to assistant director and finally to director."

If you don't have plans to pursue a degree in hotel management or a comparable course, Jackie warns that your climb to the top can take much longer. "High school graduates usually start as room attendants and move up from there." At Bally's, Kay also hires recent high school grads to work as department receptionists, office secretaries, and in other entry-level positions.

Executive housekeepers are considered part of the hotel's executive team, and are on the same level as director of food and beverages or the hotel manager. Since executive housekeepers are already at the head of their particular department, advancement possibilities are limited. Promotions are usually to other hotel departments. Kay says that she has seen many directors of housekeeping advance to higher positions such as that of general manager. "Anyone with the managerial experience of an executive housekeeper can move on."

Advancement Possibilities

Food and beverage directors *supervise all food and drinks served in the hotel by way of room service, cocktail lounges, restaurants, and banquets.*

Hotel managers *direct front of the house activities, such as the front desk, reservation, and concierge desk.*

General managers *oversee all hotel departments, their employees, and departmental activities. He or she is ultimately responsible for operation of the hotel.*

Executive housekeepers are needed in every industry where cleanliness is top priority. In fact, according to a recent salary survey done by the magazine *Executive Housekeeping Today*, hospitals account for 48 percent of employed housekeeping managers; other health care facilities, such as nursing homes or hospices, employ 15 percent; colleges and universities 8 percent; retirement facilities employ 7.4 percent. The hotel and motel industry employs only 6.3 percent of housekeeping professionals. The remaining executive housekeepers are employed by contract cleaners (3.3 percent), industrial plants (1.1 percent) manufacturers and industry suppliers (1.1 percent), government (0.3 percent), and other undefined groups (9.5 percent).

WHAT ARE SOME RELATED JOBS?

The U.S. Department of Labor classifies executive housekeepers under the heading, Service Industry Managers and Officials (DOT). Other careers classified under this heading include apartment house managers, building superintendents, managers of parks of manufactured homes, bed and breakfast managers, convention managers, executive chefs, golf club managers, recreation supervisors and superintendents, hotel and motel managers, hotel front office managers, directors of food services, food service managers, laundry superintendents, and dietary managers.

WHAT ARE THE SALARY RANGES?

According to a 1997 salary survey conducted by *Executive Housekeeping Today*, the average executive housekeeper, certified and with some college back-

Related Jobs

Apartment house managers

Bed and breakfast managers

Building superintendents

Convention managers

Dietary managers

Directors of food services

Executive chefs

Food service managers

Golf club managers

Hotel and motel managers

Hotel front office managers

Laundry superintendents

*Managers of parks of manufac-
tured homes*

*Recreation supervisors and
superintendents*

ground, can expect to earn $36,974. Top executive housekeepers can earn over $110,000 a year. Overall earnings are affected by experience, level of education, type and size of organization, and the number of employees supervised.

As part of the salary package, managers are offered health, dental, and life insurance, pension or 401K plans, and hotel and store discounts. Some hotels and resorts offer on-site living quarters, meals, and laundry services. Year-end bonuses are sometimes awarded to managers, depending on the employer.

Education plays a big role in salary. This survey also shows that those with a four-year college degree can expect to earn $18,000 more a year than those who have not earned a high school diploma. Registration or certification also makes an employee more valuable (adding about one thousand dollars to annual salaries), as does working experience.

If you want to make the most money, relocate to the East where the average housekeeping professional earns $42,281. It's tough luck, money-wise, if you live in Ohio or West Virginia—executive housekeepers there average only $28,583.

WHAT IS THE JOB OUTLOOK?

Job opportunities and salary figures for hotel housekeeping are expected to remain healthy into the next century. Several key factors, among them more international business travel, rising personal incomes, continued growth of the two-income family, and increased emphasis on leisure time and travel, contribute to this industry's bright future. It's a simple equation—the more people travel, the more lodging establishments are needed, and the higher the demand for professionals to keep house. Even if the nation's economy should dip, chances are housekeeping is last on the list of budget trimming. Without the reputation of a clean house, no hotel has a chance for success.

Education plays a pivotal role in any job search. Though work experience is important, a college degree, whether a bachelor's or associate's, will give you that winning edge. Familiarity with computers is important because much of the paperwork associated with running a department of hundreds has been replaced by various computer software programs.

The use of robotics has helped the work load of cleaners. Much of the lifting and cleaning of heavy pieces of furniture is now done by machinery. Large lobby areas are now cleaned by automatic washers instead of hand mops. Even cleaning solutions are improved to do their job faster and better, yet stay friendly to different woods and fabrics, as well as the environment. Movements and cleaning steps are constantly streamlined for efficiency and speed.

If there is a definite downside to this occupation, and to the department in general, it is the public's perception. Housekeeping is considered by many as basic blue-collar work and oftentimes looked down upon. Steps are being taken—certification, education, and standardization are a few—to give this department the more professional image it deserves.

Hotel Manager

SUMMARY

DEFINITION
Hotel *and* motel managers *are responsible for maintaining the daily operation, promotion, and policy of their lodging establishment. They oversee all staff activities, services, budgeting, buying, sales, and security.*

ALTERNATIVE JOB TITLES
General manager

SALARY RANGE
$25,000 to $45,000 to $87,000+

EDUCATIONAL REQUIREMENTS
Associate's degree; A bachelor's degree in hotel management is increasingly recommended

CERTIFICATION OR LICENSING
Not required, but it is a measure of professional achievement

EMPLOYMENT OUTLOOK
About as fast as the average

HIGH SCHOOL SUBJECTS
Business
Mathematics
Speech

PERSONAL INTERESTS
Business Management
Helping people: personal service
Selling/Making a deal

Vlato Lemick, hotel general manager, arrives at his office promptly at 8:30 AM. Armed with a large cup of coffee and a red pencil, he sits at his desk to review his schedule book and makes notes for the day.

9:00 AM—Meeting with ad rep from the *Daily Southtown* Newspaper. Highlight holiday advertising: discounted room packages, children's breakfast with Santa Claus, New Year's Eve gala.

10:30 AM—Property walk-around with Sheila, executive housekeeper. Note: Make sure pool area is free of used towels and clutter.

12 noon—Work through lunch! Meeting with department heads: housekeeping, food and beverage, catering, accounting. Business forecasting for next month. Numbers look good!

1:30 PM—Inspect water damage from last week's storm with State Farm Insurance appraiser. Note: discuss next year's insurance policy—what changes are needed?

3:00 PM—Meeting with new linen supplier. Don't forget to bring samples of napkins and sheets for comparison.

5:30 PM—Attend hotel and motel convention at McCormick Convention Center. Look for any new computer programs to organize customer database.

Vlato sighs, exhausted from reading what the day has in store. He is about to return some phone calls when his assistant comes in. "Mr. Lemick, a guest is complaining about his folio charges, and he wants to see the manager. Do you have time to take care of this?"

"Sure. Of course I do," Vlato responds. "It's part of my job."

WHAT DOES A HOTEL MANAGER DO?

A hotel general manager is like the ringmaster of a circus. He has to manage several tasks simultaneously, giving each department individual but equal attention, all the while making sure the guests are happy and satisfied. Does this sound like an easy job? Think again.

A general manager is responsible for the overall supervision of the hotel, the different departments, and their staff. He follows operating guidelines set by the hotel's owners, or if part of a chain, to the hotel's main headquarters and executive board. A general manager, also known as the GM, allocates funds to all departments of the hotel, approves expenditures, sets room rates, and establishes standards for food and beverage service, hotel decor, and all guest services. GMs tour the hotel property every day, usually with the head of the housekeeping department, to make certain the hotel is kept clean and orderly. GMs are responsible for keeping the hotel's accounting books in order, advertising, room sales, inventory, and ordering of supplies, as well as interviewing and training of new employees. However, in larger hotels, the GM is usually supported by one or more assistants.

Did you know . . .

There are over 99,000 managers working in the hotel industry.

80% of all managers are male; 20% female.

Hotel managers work an average of 55 hours a week.

Over 70% of managers describe their average work-day as "exhausting."

The average tenure of a hotel manager is 6.7 years.

Some hotels still employ *resident managers.* Such managers live at the hotel and are on call virtually twenty four hours a day, in cases of emergencies. Resident managers work a regular eight-hour shift, attending to the duties of the hotel. In many modern hotels, the general manager has taken the place of resident managers.

Front office managers supervise the activity and staff of the front desk. They are responsible for directing reservations and sleeping room assignments. Front office managers make sure that all guests are treated courteously, and check-in and check-out periods are managed smoothly. Any guest complaints or problems are usually directed to the front desk first—managers are responsible for rectifying all criticisms before they reach the general manager.

The *personnel manager* heads the human resources or personnel department. He or she is responsible for hiring and firing employees and works with other personnel employees such as *employee relations managers* to protect employee rights and address grievances.

Restaurant managers oversee the daily operation of hotel restaurants. They manage employees such as waiters and waitresses, busboys and -girls, hosts and hostesses, bartenders, and cooks and bakers. They are responsible for customer complaints and satisfaction. *Food and beverage managers* are responsible for all food service operations in the hotel—from restaurants, cocktail lounges and banquets to room service. They supervise food and service quality and preparation, order supplies from different vendors, and estimate food costs.

Hotels can profit by marketing their facilities for conventions, meetings, and special events. Such hotels may have a *convention services manager* in charge of coordinating such activities. He or she takes care of all necessary details such as blocking sleeping rooms and arranging meeting rooms or ballrooms. The convention services manager is responsible for resolving any problems that arise.

Executive housekeepers are managers who supervise the work of the room attendants, housekeepers, janitors, gardeners, and the laundry staff. Depending on the size and structure of the hotel, they may also be in charge of ordering cleaning supplies, linens, towels, and toiletries. Some executive housekeepers may be responsible for dealing with suppliers and vendors.

WHAT IS IT LIKE TO BE A HOTEL MANAGER?

When asked what made him enter this career, Vlato Lemick has a quick and simple answer. "I grew up in the industry." Literally. Vlato's parents owned a hotel, and the business became a family affair.

Training started early. "I worked all the desks," Vlato recalls. "From the time I was in grade school, I was helping out at the front desk, answering the switchboard, cleaning rooms, doing lawn maintenance. I even did some plumbing."

After high school, Vlato left hospitality and studied aeronautical engineering. He established a career in the airline industry, but found it unstable—many airlines were merging or going out of business. Vlato soon decided to return to the family business and came to work at the hotel. Years later, Vlato is now the general manager and owner of three hotels—a Holiday Inn and two Hampton Inns.

A typical day is a busy one for Vlato. "I spend a lot of time returning phone calls. I deal with all sorts of people from insurance agents to accountants. I also do business forecasts to get an idea of how many guests are expected." These forecasts are very important, not only to the general manager, but to other departmental managers as well.

The property walk-around is on Vlato's daily list of things to do. He, along with the head of housekeeping, tours the hotel, inside and out. They take note of the cleanliness and order of the lobby, pool area, elevator banks, and other common areas. Sections that are not up to the hotel's standards are noted to the proper department and closely observed on the next day's property tour.

One of the least rewarding aspects of Vlato's job is dealing with customer complaints. "Problems do reach my desk, and I have to take care of them." Does he only give attention to the important problems? "No," he says firmly. "No complaint or request should be considered unimportant." Does he find his job rewarding? "Definitely. I strive to keep all my hotels operational and successful." People interaction is also very important to him. "I like knowing that my staff has high morale—and low turnover."

//I like knowing that my staff has high morale—and low turnover."

Vlato also enjoys the variety of tasks that come with the position—no day is ever the same. He recalls one of the strangest incidents of his career. "I once had guests that wanted to hold a party in a room. They refused my offer of the complimentary party room and instead complained. Why were there beds in their sleeping room? Why couldn't we remove these beds from their rooms!? They were simply unreasonable. I ended up asking them to leave the hotel. No, they were not rowdy students on prom night—they were middle-aged mothers and their daughters at a cheerleading convention!" All in a day's work.

HAVE I GOT WHAT IT TAKES TO BE A HOTEL MANAGER?

Hotel managers are strong leaders, with a flair for organization, communication and, most importantly, working well with other people. If this description fits your personality, great; if you lack two or more of these traits, then maybe this is the wrong career path for you.

Because general managers must supervise all departments in the hotel, it is imperative that they be able to work with different types of people, situations, and temperaments. Good managers should initiate, implement, and

To be a successful hotel manager, you should:

Have strong leadership, organizational, and communication skills

Be able to work with different types of people, situations, and temperaments.

Be a good problem-solver and be attentive to details

Be a born diplomat, especially when handling guest complaints

Be willing to work long hours, including late nights, weekends, and holidays

praise the work of their staffs. In order to keep the hotel running smoothly, general managers need to establish policies and procedures and make certain their directions are carried out. They must be able to solve problems and concentrate on details, whether large or small. It is a stressful job and managers need to keep a cool demeanor when dealing with difficult situations that come their way. Managers must be born diplomats, especially when handling guest complaints. They need to validate all criticisms, no matter how trivial, and find the fastest and most satisfying solution to the problem.

Do you hope to have a nine-to-five work-day? You won't have one with this career. General managers usually work an average of fifty-five hours a week. Weekends and holidays are no exceptions. Even if off duty, managers can be called back to work in cases of emergency—night or day.

HOW DO I BECOME A HOTEL MANAGER?

EDUCATION

High School

It's a good idea to begin preparing for a career in hotel management while in high school. Concentrate on a business-oriented curriculum, with classes in finance, accounting, and mathematics. Since computers are widely used in the hotel setting for reservations, accounting, and management of supplies, computer literacy is important. Brush up on your speaking skills while in high school—you'll need them when giving direction and supervision to a large and diverse staff. A second language—especially Spanish or French, even Japanese—will be very helpful to you in the future.

Instead of working at the mall or local fast-food outlet, play it smart and consider obtaining part-time or seasonal work at a local hotel. The hotels owned and managed by Vlato employ many high school students to work the switchboard and front desk, and as members of banquet, restaurant, and housekeeping staff. In addition to making money, these teenagers are getting valuable experience and making useful contacts for future employment. Check with your high school career center if they post employment opportunities in your area. Don't forget that career centers, your local library, and the Internet can all be helpful when researching college programs or specific businesses.

Postsecondary Training

Many companies require management trainees to have a minimum of a bachelor's degree in hotel and restaurant management. There are over 150 colleges and universities that offer undergraduate and graduate programs in hotel administration. Many community colleges and technical schools—over 800 nationwide—also have two-year courses in hotel management.

A typical hotel management program will concentrate on hotel administration, food service management, accounting, economics, marketing, housekeeping, computers, and hotel maintenance engineering. To complement class instruction, most programs require students to work on site at a hotel. Some universities, such as the famed Cornell School of Hospitality, have a training hotel on campus. Many hotels will also consider candidates with degrees in business management, public relations, or other related fields, if they are highly qualified and talented.

//My part-time jobs for cash during school suddenly turned into a career opportunity I hadn't really considered."—Susan Lee, front office manager for the Radisson Plaza Hotel Minneapolis, on her decision to enter the hotel and motel industry.

WHO WILL HIRE ME?

Because Vlato more or less grew up in the business, it seemed logical for him to work in a hotel. After working as an aeronautical engineer for a variety of airlines, he missed the employment stability of the hotel industry. His first real job (not counting the many hotel jobs he held as a teenager) was back at his parents' hotel.

Unless you are lucky to have family already in the business, you'll have to do some future planning and maybe pound the pavement a little. If you are looking for a job to lay the groundwork for college, then start with your school's career center or your guidance counselor. They may be privy to such job openings. Also, consider looking in your community paper under "Hotel," "Motel," "Restaurant," or "Business." It may be a good idea to call local hotels, or even restaurants, to see if they are hiring for seasonal work.

College seniors can make job inquiries with their school's placement office. Usually such centers will try to match a student's skills and education with the right position. Many schools also hold job fairs where prospective employers can set up immediate interviews to qualified candidates. Make sure you dress professionally, and have copies of your resume ready to circulate. Not all companies send recruiters to campus job fairs, in which case you can send your resume directly to their human resource department. Make the extra effort of finding out who is in charge of hiring, so your cover letter won't read "Dear Sir or Madam."

Some major employers in the hotel industry are Comfort Inn, based in Newark, Delaware; the Hilton Hotels, based in Carolton, Texas; and Mirage Resorts of Las Vegas, which is noted for its quality of management. Host Marriott Corporation offers a fast-track management program for qualified employees, and has been known to encourage career advancement for minorities and women employees. This feature can be very beneficial for women interested in this career. The field is currently dominated by men—only 20 percent of hotel managers are women.

Vlato also stresses the importance of long-term experience in this industry. He suggests working at least one year at a company before moving to another. Vlato looks at that detail when it comes to hiring new employees. He questions applicants who for example, have had more than four employers in less than two years.

Books and Magazines About the Industry

Professionals Read:

Hosteur

Marketing Review

Lodging

Try Reading:

The Hotel: Backstairs at the World's Most Exclusive Hotel, *by Jeffrey Robinson*

Make Your Mark in the Hotel Industry, *by Rosemary Grebel and Phyllis Pogrund*

The Hotel and Restaurant Business, *by Donald E. Lundberg*

The Spirit to Serve, *by J. Willard Marriott and Kathi Ann Brown*

WHERE CAN I GO FROM HERE?

Where does Vlato see himself in the next ten years? "I would like to own more hotels," he says assuredly. Most hotels are part of a chain, with many offered as franchise business opportunities. Each franchise hotel is run according to specifications and recommendations, such as management and pricing, offered by the parent company. With Vlato's experience and ambition he could easily handle the responsibility of running more Holiday Inn hotels.

The position of general manager is among the top rungs of the hotel career ladder. It's unlikely this would be your first industry job. In the past, employees could advance from the front desk, housekeeping, or food and beverage departments, or even the sales staff. Good experience and hard work was sufficient to move ahead. However, in today's highly technical age, together with a competitive work force, experience, though still important, is not enough for job advancement. Most candidates have some postsecondary education; many have at least a bachelor's degree in hotel and restaurant management. Graduates entering the hotel industry usually pay their dues by working as assistant hotel managers, assistant departmental managers, or shift managers. Many hotels, such as the Marriott or Hilton hotels, have specific management training programs for their management-bound employees. Employees are encouraged to work different desks so they will be knowledgeable about each department of the hotel.

The average tenure of a hotel general manager is about six and a half years; those who have worked as a GM for ten years or more usually view their job as a lifetime commitment. Managers who leave the profession usually advance to the regional or even national area of hotel management, such as property management or the administrative or financial positions of the hotel chain. Some, like Vlato, may opt to open their own hotel franchise, or even operate a small inn or bed and breakfast establishment. The management skills learned as a general manager are valuable, and can be successfully utilized in any avenue of business.

Advancement possibilities

Regional operations managers *travel throughout a specific geographic region to see that hotel chain members are operated and maintained according to the guidelines and standards set by the company.*

Branch operations managers *reorganize hotels that are doing poorly financially, or set up a new hotel operation.*

Owners *of an inn or bed and breakfast establishment are called* **proprietors.** *They are responsible for every aspect of the business—from setup, advertising, ordering supplies and food to guest relations.*

WHAT ARE SOME RELATED JOBS?

The U.S. Department of Labor classifies hotel managers under the heading Service Industry Managers and Officials. Other careers listed under this heading include apartment house managers, aquatic facility managers, building superintendents, camp directors, executive housekeepers, convention managers, casino managers, golf club managers, health club managers, hospital administrators, recreation center managers, food service managers, restaurant managers, hotel recreational facilities managers, and travel agency managers.

WHAT ARE THE SALARY RANGES?

Salary figures vary according to the worker's level of expertise, the lodging establishment, the duties involved, and of course, the location of the hotel. General managers working in larger urban hotels can expect to have a larger staff to supervise than a smaller inn in rural areas. A 1996 National Association of Colleges and Employers study found the average starting offer to graduates with a bachelor's degree in hotel management to be $25,000 a year.

According to a recent hospitality industry salary survey conducted by Roth Young, hotel general managers, depending on their experience, can make anywhere from $45,000 annually at hotels with 150 rooms or less, to $87,000 or more a year at hotels with over 350 rooms. Some managers can also boost their annual income with company year-end bonuses—up to 25 percent of their base salary. These bonuses are based on the hotel's profits for the year. Among other job perks are lodging and meal discounts, free parking, and laundry. Salaries of assistant managers vary depending on the department in question. According to the same Roth Young study, front office managers earn an average of $28,000 a year, assistant hotel managers about $40,000 a year, while food and beverage managers average $43,000 a year. All managers receive paid holidays and vacations, sick leave, and other benefits such as medical and life insurance, pension or profit-sharing plans, and educational assistance.

Related Jobs

Apartment house managers
Aquatic facility managers
Building superintendents
Camp directors
Casino managers
Convention managers
Executive housekeepers
Food service managers
Golf club managers
Health club manager
Hospital administrators
Hotel recreational facilities managers
Recreation center managers
Restaurant managers
Travel agency managers

WHAT IS THE JOB OUTLOOK?

The job outlook for hotel managers continues to be bright through the year 2006. Business travel continues to increase, as does domestic travel for the private sector. As the demand grows, so does the need for lodging establishments and qualified people to manage them. However, the number of jobs for hotel managers is not expected to grow as rapidly as in the past. Travelers are now looking for bargains and no-frills type of lodging. To meet the demand, many hotel chains are offering a larger choice of economy properties, which as a rule, do not have many of the amenities found in luxury hotels, such as in-room food and beverage service and in-house restaurants. Because there are fewer departments, fewer managers are needed to manage these hotels.

Newly built hotels and luxury or resort properties will continue to need well trained and experienced managerial employees. Many job openings will also result from current managers moving to other positions or occupations, retiring, or leaving the work force for other reasons. Employment and advancement opportunities will be best for those with college degrees in hotel or restaurant management, or a similar business degree. Managers with excellent work experience will be in demand, as well as those who have successfully completed certification requirements. As hotels and motels become more computer-dependent for many duties and functions, familiarity with different computer programs will be key.

Hotel Restaurant Manager

SUMMARY

DEFINITION
Hotel restaurant managers oversee the complete operation of a restaurant. They recruit and train staff, keep inventory of food supplies, handle customer complaints, and prepare the menu. They may also supervise the activities of the hotel's main restaurant as well as the cocktail lounge, banquets, and any food ordered through room service.

ALTERNATIVE JOB TITLES
Food and beverage manager

SALARY RANGE
$24,700 to $30,000 to $46,000+

EDUCATIONAL REQUIREMENTS
High school diploma; Bachelor's degree

CERTIFICATION OR LICENSING
Recommended

EMPLOYMENT OUTLOOK
Faster than the average

HIGH SCHOOL SUBJECTS
Business
English (writing/literature)
Mathematics

PERSONAL INTERESTS
Business management
Cooking
Helping people: personal service
Travel

It's 11:30 AM, the height of the morning rush. Servers are moving quickly, taking orders. They move on to check guests at another table, stopping to top off their coffees. Dining-room attendants work quietly but efficiently, clearing dishes off a table and dressing it for the next group. The breakfast buffet is neat and orderly despite the nearly three hundred customers who have been served so far this morning. The hostess is busy showing a large group with children to a far corner table. An attendant follows with two booster seats and a high chair.

From where restaurant manager Roberta Jackson is standing, she has a perfect view of the floor. It seems a normal morning, she thinks to herself. Busy, and just on the edge of chaotic.

"What do you mean I've been denied?? You must be wrong. Try the card again!"

Roberta is there in an instant. "Hello, I'm Roberta Jackson, the hotel restaurant manager. Can I be of assistance?" Ten minutes and two credit cards later, the customer is comforted ("Somehow, you must have demagnetized your card strip. An alligator wallet maybe?"). The waitress was well tipped, and most importantly, the matter resolved. Roberta breathes a sigh of relief—at least until the next mini-crisis.

WHAT DOES A HOTEL RESTAURANT MANAGER DO?

The value of a good conductor to an orchestra is what a restaurant manager is to a hotel's food service department. Both are necessary in gathering groups of people together—each with a different responsibility or task—and having them work as a single unit. The efficient and profitable management of a hotel restaurant falls on the shoulders of its restaurant manager.

In a hotel or motel environment, the restaurant manager oversees the many duties involving food service—from restaurants or cafes housed inside the hotel, the cocktail lounges, and sometimes, the room service department. In larger hotels and motels, the restaurant manager may receive help from one or more *assistant managers* and *executive chefs*. Assistant managers supervise the dining rooms and other areas of food management, as needed. Executive chefs oversee operations in the kitchen, from food preparation to final presentation. *Bookkeepers* are sometimes hired to help with administrative details. Assistant managers, executive chefs, and bookkeepers report to the restaurant manager. However, especially in smaller lodging places, the restaurant manager is expected to perform with very little support.

A very important duty of the restaurant manager is the ordering and receiving of supplies. On a daily basis, the restaurant manager must check and monitor food consumption, then place orders with different vendors as needed. To have enough fresh fruits, vegetables, and meats, such perishable foodstuffs may be ordered many times during the week. Deliveries need to consistently meet the hotel's standard of quality. Supplies of linens, tableware, cooking and serving utensils, cleaning supplies, as well as larger items such as furniture and fixtures, are kept in order by the manager.

No food establishment would succeed without competent and hardworking servers, cooks, dining-room attendants, and hosts.

Lingo to Learn

Clearing or busing: The removal of tableware, equipment, or debris.

The Floor: The dining area of a restaurant.

Forecasting: A business tool used to estimate the number of guests the hotel is expecting for the next few days. This amount will help determine food demand.

Multifaceted Food Delivery System (MFDS): An eating establishment that is able to produce and serve a broad range of menu items. Hotel restaurants are examples of MFDS.

Servers: The waiters and waitresses working in a restaurant.

Workstations: The group of dining tables assigned to a waiter or waitress to serve.

Interviewing, hiring, training, and even firing these workers are additional vital functions of the restaurant manager. Weekly work schedules are made to ensure coverage during peak dining times, while giving all employees equal and fair hours of work.

Administrative work is another primary obligation of the restaurant manager. Accurate hourly work records, wages, and taxes are some examples of paperwork needed to prepare payrolls. Managers must also keep tallies of supplies and equipment ordered and received. Computers have eased the workload tremendously in the past few years. Software, such as the Point-of-Service System (POS), allows for restaurants to keep track of employee productivity as well as sale progress of menu items. Using a POS system, the waiter or waitress inputs the diner's menu order where it is immediately sent to the kitchen for preparation. The same information is used by the computer to total food and beverage orders into the final check. If the customer is paying with a credit card, the POS system can immediately verify the card number. Many managers use the POS system's daily tallies of food and drinks ordered to keep inventory supplies well stocked and current. Sometimes, additional supplies are ordered from specific vendors using this system.

Supervision of the dining rooms and kitchen is not as simple as it sounds. Food must be prepared, presented, and served correctly, but also in a timely manner. The kitchen staff must meet government regulations on sanitary standards of food preparation. Managers may meet with the chef regularly to analyze recipes for ingredients, portion size, labor, and overhead costs to assign a menu price. Menus need to be updated from time to time, and additional supplies ordered ahead of time for new menu items.

However, not all duties of the restaurant manager are exciting or pleasant. They also receive and resolve customer complaints in a professional manner, even if the criticisms come at the busiest and most inopportune time. Managers must be versatile enough to be able to pitch in where help is needed most—seating guests, serving food, clearing tables, or taking food orders. They are among the first to arrive at the hotel restaurant and most often do not leave until all sales receipts are tallied, equipment shut down, lights dimmed, and alarm systems started.

WHAT IS IT LIKE TO BE A HOTEL RESTAURANT MANAGER?

Roberta Jackson's workday starts very early—5:30 AM. As manager for Allie's Restaurant, an eatery housed inside the Marriott Hotel in downtown Chicago, she's always one of the first to arrive in order to get ready for the breakfast crowd. "I go in and get the operation ready for the day, and make sure my support staff is there and doing what they need to do for the day. I get my banks [registers] ready. I start setting up the floor [the dining room], so my servers know where they are going. I give them their workstations [assigned dining tables] for the day, as well as their side work duties."

There is coffee to brew, breads and butters to gather, the breakfast buffet to assemble, as well as a dozen other details to iron out before 6:30 AM, when Allie's opens its doors for breakfast. That's a lot to do in an hour!

"Allie's is a high-volume restaurant. We can do about three to five hundred from the hours between 6:30 to 11:00 AM. We have a breakfast buffet and we also run off the menu."

Although breakfast service ends around 11:00 AM, there may be no time for a break. Roberta usually schedules a short menu class for servers who need the review, or a general staff training class. After this is done, there is definitely no time for a breather. It's lunchtime!

> *II* Don't ever prejudge a situation; keep yourself open. That way you can learn many things to enhance yourself for the next day."

"We go directly into lunch and the lunch buffet—I have my buffet attendants set that up, I try to get my servers out for a thirty-minute break and go into lunch. Lunch runs from 11:00 AM to around 2:00 PM." Roberta laughs when asked at what time she takes a lunch break. "Somewhere in there! Somewhere between 10:00 and 11:00 is when we have a slow period. If I'm going to have a bite to eat, it's usually around then."

After her shift's portion of the lunch service, Roberta makes sure that her attendants have done their closing side work. She also needs to start preparing the restaurant for the mid-shift and begin prep work for the dinner service. There are so many tasks to finish before Roberta turns over the restaurant to the evening manager around 3:00 or 3:30 PM—workstations cleaned, servers' shifts ended, registers closed for the morning, among others. "If I need to do some scheduling, or order controllables, or anything I didn't get to during the day, I would do them at that time." Schedules are made weekly, from

Saturday to Saturday, giving attention to fair hours, but also to requested days off and vacations.

Forecasting is another important task managers like Roberta need to do every few days. This involves getting an estimated number of total sleeping rooms reserved for the next few days, the number of guests expected, and how many of them are committed to banquet and conference meals. This forecast helps managers estimate how many guests may be expected to take meals within the hotel's restaurants, and order supplies accordingly.

Maintaining payroll and timesheets, employee evaluations, meeting with vendors, dealing with disgruntled customers, and occasionally employees, are also other tasks for which hotel restaurant managers are responsible—not to mention the mountain of paperwork that seems to come with the territory. Keeping up to date on the industry is important as well. Restaurant professionals read trade publications such as *Lodging, Hosteur,* and *Restaurant Hospitality*. Conventions are great opportunities for managers to learn of new developments in their field. One example is the National Restaurant and Hotel Convention held annually at different locations through the United States. If there is a shortage of staff, or if the restaurant is particularly busy, then good managers have been known to grab an apron and pitch in where needed—whether taking orders, busing tables, or peeling shrimp in the prep kitchen.

This is a tough industry. Being a hotel restaurant manager can be taxing, both physically and mentally. The key to success is to remain calm and level headed no matter how tough the day, uncooperative the employee, or irate the customer. Roberta advises, "Don't ever prejudge a situation; keep yourself open. That way you can learn many things to enhance yourself for the next day."

HAVE I GOT WHAT IT TAKES TO BE A RESTAURANT MANAGER?

Let's be brutally honest. If you look forward to lazy Sunday afternoons, consecutive days off, or picture-perfect family holidays, then this job is definitely not for you. Because of the nature of the work—the long hours and the commitment of opening a hotel restaurant on time, often seven days a week—quality of life can certainly be lacking. Managers are the backbone of a successful eatery, so many times they are called on to work weekends and holidays. It would be safe to say their lives revolve around the restaurant, the hotel, and the demands of business.

Hours are long and stressful, but a good manager needs to set the example as a courteous, hard-working, and cheerful employee, no matter how demanding (read: irritating) the customer might be. The restaurant manager is usually the person to field customer complaints. "Well, that's the nature of the business," Roberta Jackson admits. The old adage "the customer is always right," is the rule in these situations. She stresses that a manager's job is not to judge, but to listen, be understanding, and try to calm and please the customer. Roberta Jackson uses cases of customer complaints as a tool to help herself and her staff train for the future.

To be a successful hotel restaurant manager, you should:

Have good people skills in order to work with co-workers and address customer inquiries and complaints

Have leadership and motivational skills

Be organized and attentive to detail

Be willing to work long hours, including weekends and holidays

A rotating schedule may be hard to live with, but there are definite up-sides to this career. What is the most rewarding aspect of Roberta's job? "Having a restaurant that is functioning smoothly, satisfied customers, and a satisfied staff. If I keep that flow going, if I can keep my staff happy and productive, if I can make sure they have the tools that they need in order to make the guest happy, then everyone is complementing each other. Once that gets going, then of course it's complementing me, and that makes me happy." With a revolving morning staff of fifteen servers and a support staff of sixteen, hundreds of hungry customers, and at least seven ways to cook an egg, it is no easy task for Roberta.

HOW DO I BECOME A HOTEL RESTAURANT MANAGER?

EDUCATION

High School

The food and beverage department is one of the best places to start in the hotel industry since there are so many positions to fill. Many entry-level food service jobs may lead to better-paying and more responsible positions if the worker shows enough drive and potential.

You can prepare for a career in hotel restaurant management by taking a wide range of classes, especially business, English, and communication courses. Home economics classes would also be helpful. Vince Vito, a food and beverage manager for Hyatt Hotels in Oak Brook, Illinois, is the manager of

Anthony's Chop House and Foxes Sports Grill, both hotel restaurants. He found his high school marketing and business administration classes helpful in preparing for his career.

Many hotels and motels are willing to hire students like yourself to work banquets, as waiters, waitresses, dining-room attendants, or inside the kitchen. This would provide working experience in the field of food service, as well as a way to earn good spending money.

Vince had the foresight to begin part-time hotel work while a senior in high school. His job title was bellman, but was not limited to carrying luggage. "I was working all over the hotel—from the banquet room, to the front desk, to getting toothbrushes for hotel guests." He recommends that high school students find hotel work in any capacity, just to get valuable experience.

Postsecondary Training

In today's competitive market, many hotels and motels are placing stricter educational requirements on their new employees, and are able to choose from a large pool of recent graduates. Most hotels prefer management trainees from two- or four-year college programs, especially graduates from a hospitality management program. However, students with other degrees may still be hired if they show interest and aptitude in the hotel business.

The best bet when it comes to education is a bachelor's degree in restaurant and food service management. There are over 170 colleges and universities offering various programs in restaurant and hotel management, as well as institutional food service management. Associate degrees or formal certificates can be earned at one of 800 community or junior colleges, and technical institutes in the United States.

According to the Council on Hotel, Restaurant and Institutional Education (CHRIE), a successful hospitality program will consist of four main areas: major classes, general education and advanced learning skills, electives, and work experience—also known as laboratory work. Vince recalls, "For one class, we had to go to a cafeteria and begin cooking breakfast for about five hundred students."

College students interested in management usually study business administration combined with food service or home economics. Many hotels start university-trained employees as assistant managers. In Vince's case, his college marketing class, business systems, nutrition, and food preparation classes have been helpful to his career. He also joined the Club Managers Association while attending Eastern Illinois University.

As always, it pays to have the advantage of work experience to back up a solid education. Part-time or seasonal work in a hotel's food service department during college will be a definite foot in the door come interview time.

CERTIFICATION

Certification in the hotel food service industry is not mandatory but definitely a recognized and respected achievement. A status of being an experienced employee, and knowledgeable of the industry standards, comes with certification. The Education Institute of the American Hotel and Motel Association, among other institutions, offers certification programs to all levels of hotel employment—from entry-level positions to upper management. Those in the food service industry would most likely strive to be a Certified Food and Beverage Executive (CFBE), Foodservice Management Professional (FMP), or perhaps a Certified Hotel Administrator (CHA), or Certified Lodging Manager (CLM). At the Chicago Marriott, "bands" and "grades" measure not only Roberta's experience and expertise, but they also serve as a guide for pay scales.

According to the Education Institute, eligibility for certification can be achieved two ways—through emphasis on education or experience. A letter of recommendation from a superior and successful completion of a certification exam covering the hotel, and food and beverage industry is needed. Designees are recertified every five years based on their accomplishments, and are awarded new lapel pins and certificates reflecting the number of years certified. The appropriate certification designation is used on letterheads, business cards, and other documentation.

Employees certified in their field are in demand for promotion, and are good candidates for other positions within the hotel industry.

WHO WILL HIRE ME?

Roberta's introduction to the hospitality industry was anything but conventional. Circumstances in life forced her to make a career change from working as a research technician to her present field. Roberta received her training for this position the hard way—working her way up through the ranks. She began her career as a hostess, working her way to operational supervisor for banquets, to restaurant assistant manager to restaurant manager.

It was all about seizing opportunity. "I discovered this market (the hotel industry) was wide open. I started investigating it and found this was something I could grow in and enjoy doing so." Her natural ability for the hotel trade was sparked earlier in life, when she ran a guest house and gave tours for her guests while living in Liberia.

Her formal training has been thanks to hard work and strong support from the Marriott Corporation. "Marriott does an excellent job preparing you for your current position, and those you would like to obtain," Roberta says. Is this offered to everyone? "Of course it depends on the individual. Also, the kind of rating you receive when you are reviewed. If you show you are a star in the area you are working, then of course you are looked at and approached for extra training and advancement."

Job openings are posted everywhere—at job fairs, in hotel trade magazines, and in newspapers. You should look in the job classifieds under the headings "Hotel," "Motel," "Hospitality," "Restaurant Manager," or perhaps "Resorts." National organizations are great sources of information for jobs. Check with the National Restaurant Association or the American Hotel and Motel Association for information, or better yet, log on to their Web sites for job descriptions and openings nationwide. Don't forget to use the resources any regional or state lodging association may have to offer (look in the phone book for associations in your area). Remember that summer you worked as a dining room attendant at the local Holiday Inn? Now is the time to get in touch with contacts you made at the time. If you worked hard and showed initiative, your supervisors will remember you and perhaps act as references.

Vince found his position at a job fair where many hotels were recruiting, Hyatt Hotels among them. "It was towards the end of my senior year at Eastern Illinois University, and Hyatt had an immediate opening for operations supervisor. They needed someone right away, so I didn't give it another thought, but passed out my resume anyway. Later, I received a call for an opening in their food and beverage department." Most of his university classmates have found good jobs in the hospitality industry right away, many in the cities of their choice. Not many graduates needed the assistance of headhunters—companies that match your job skills and education to companies. This may be the best example of the edge hospitality program graduates have over other candidates. Vince stresses that while it is possible to move up the ranks without a degree, "it's difficult to advance without education."

WHERE CAN I GO FROM HERE?

Where does Roberta see herself in the next ten years? "Marriott has another division called Management Services. I would like to go into that division and work as a manager there. These are the managers that run cafeterias, banks, hospitals."

Industrial food service is a fast-growing arm of a hotel's food and beverage department, especially accounts with health care or assisted-living institutions. The industrial side is not necessarily a more profitable employer, but the hours are more stable, usually nine to five, and—unless special projects or events are planned—weekends and holidays are free. "It does allow for more quality of life," Roberta stresses.

Another logical work path is the job of restaurant director. This position would supervise the overall management of food service within the hotel. Restaurant managers report to the restaurant director.

Many experienced hotel restaurant managers are promoted to the executive side of hotel management. Holding the responsibility of running a business that contributes large revenues to the hotel make restaurant managers good candidates for higher rungs on the corporate ladder.

While most hotel restaurant managers stay within the boundaries of hotel management, a few do venture out to start their own restaurants and cafes. The rigorous training they receive at the hotel is invaluable when establishing a business.

Advancement possibilities

Hotel general managers *manage and direct all hotel departments, their activities and employees.*

Hotel managers *are in charge of the activities and employees of the front, reservation, and concierge desks.*

Industrial food and beverage managers *handle food service for businesses, school, and other organizations and institutions.*

Restaurant directors *supervise all food service and restaurant activity.*

WHAT ARE SOME RELATED JOBS?

The U.S. Department of Labor classifies hotel restaurant manager under the heading, Service Industry Managers and Officials (DOT). Also under this heading are people who work alongside the hotel restaurant manager such as the *assistant restaurant manager* and the *executive chef.* They help with managerial duties on the dining floor and in the kitchen. Other related jobs within the hotel industry's food and beverage department are *banquet managers* and *catering managers.* Both are responsible for supervising the food served in the hotel's banquet facilities and conference rooms. *Industrial food managers,* many employed by larger hotel chains, serve institutions such as hospitals, schools, businesses, and nursing homes.

Other careers classified under this heading include bed and breakfast managers, convention managers, bowling alley managers, golf club managers,

hotel and motel managers, casino managers, cocktail lounge managers, hotel recreational facilities managers, hotel front office managers, directors of food services, and dietary managers.

Related Jobs

Banquet managers
Bed and breakfast managers
Casino managers
Catering managers
Cocktail lounge managers
Convention managers
Directors of food services
Executive chefs
Hotel front office managers
Hotel recreational facilities managers

WHAT ARE THE SALARY RANGES?

Salaries in this industry are dependent on the location and size of property. Higher-paying jobs are found in urban areas where hotels and motels tend to be larger. Certain geographical areas of the United States also offer more pay, in some part to offset the high cost of living in an area such as Hawaii or New York.

According to *Comparison for Salaried Persons in Food Service*, a book published by the National Restaurant Association, 1996 salaries for hotel restaurant unit managers start at $24,700, median at $30,000, and some top managers earning over $46,000. Benefit packages include health, and sometimes dental, insurance, savings plans as well as 401K or pension plans. Some companies offer bonus incentives. Both Hyatt Hotels and Marriott offer discounted employee rates for lodging and food. Hyatt gives each employee, regardless of rank, twelve free nights a year at any Hyatt Hotel.

WHAT IS THE JOB OUTLOOK?

Job opportunities and salary figures in the hotel restaurant trade are expected to remain healthy into the next century. Several key factors, among them rising personal incomes, continued growth of the two-income family, and increased emphasis on leisure time, contribute to this industry's bright future. According to a study conducted by the National Restaurant Association, projected sales for hotel restaurants in the United States will be about sixteen billion dollars in 1997.

No business is fully immune to the cycles of the economy. Of course, people will spend more money on luxuries if they are able. However, the activity of dining out is no longer considered a treat, but a necessity due to today's busy and hectic schedules. Many people simply do not have time to fix traditional dinners, or even a desire to do so.

What is threatening to a restaurant's measure of success is competition—and hotel restaurants are not immune to this. So many new eateries open yearly, each with a new niche or gimmick, that the market is almost saturated. Established restaurants survive by consistently giving diners good service along with good food. Hotel restaurants have a slight edge in that their expected profit margin is not as large as those of free-standing restaurants. Restaurants, especially those that serve breakfast, will always exist as a courtesy service to their hotel guests.

Computers are quickly becoming important tools in the industry. In the food and beverage department, they help with order taking, keeping inventory, ordering supplies directly from vendors, as well as making the mountain of paperwork less tedious. If you have experience with computers, specifically software developed for the restaurant industry, that's a definite advantage.

A willingness to relocate will be helpful if you are interested in managing a hotel restaurant. As a rule, better wages and opportunities for advancement are found in larger hotels located in larger cities. The downside to this? Busy urban areas like New York City, San Francisco, or Miami usually carry a higher cost of living than say, Pekin, Illinois.

The long hours and strenuous work result in a high turnover rate. This, in addition to employees leaving the work force for retirement or other reasons, will create many new job openings. Hotels and resorts being built in tourist-friendly areas like Las Vegas and Orlando will also add to the demand for good employees.

Education will be a big factor for the success of future hotel restaurant managers. Many hotel trainees are graduates of hotel, restaurant, or food service management programs, so be ready for intense competition for jobs. Why not get a summer job as banquet help or a restaurant server? The contacts you make now will be invaluable in the years to come.

Any advice for future hotel restaurant managers? Vince and Roberta stress a strong educational background coupled with solid working experience. They should know—both are successful professionals in their field.

Pilot

SUMMARY

DEFINITION
Pilots who work in travel and tourism fly aircraft that carry passengers to and from various destinations. Other pilots may work for governmental agencies or medical facilities or be involved in transporting cargo or agricultural work.

ALTERNATIVE JOB TITLES
Aircraft pilot
Airline pilot
Charter pilot
Private pilot

SALARY RANGE
$15,000 to $76,800 to $200,000

EDUCATIONAL REQUIREMENTS
High school diploma; Bachelor's degree

CERTIFICATION OR LICENSING
Mandatory

EMPLOYMENT OUTLOOK
About as fast as the average

HIGH SCHOOL SUBJECTS
Mathematics
Physics
Shop (Trade/vo-tech education)

PERSONAL INTERESTS
Airplanes
Figuring out how things work
Fixing things
Travel

It's a beautiful spring morning. The air is clean and crisp and there isn't a cloud in the sky. Mike Eckstein is behind the controls of a plane that is gently lifting into the air. He thinks back to when he was a child and dreamed of doing this very thing. Now, he does it every day—and gets paid for it.

More importantly for Mike, he's doing something he really enjoys. His job of working for an airline charter company is interesting and never routine; he never knows what to expect from week to week, or even day to day.

"This job is never normal," he says. "It's always different."

WHAT DOES A PILOT DO?

Pilots who work in travel and tourism fly aircraft that transport passengers. While there are several other kinds of pilots—such as agricultural pilots, military pilots, helicopter pilots who fly for law enforcement agencies and hospitals, and pilots who fly planes carrying cargo—this chapter will focus on pilots who fly commercial and charter aircraft.

Commercial pilots, who fly for major airlines such as United and American, are the best known and largest group of professional pilots. There are three main designations of commercial airline pilots: *captain, copilot,* and *flight engineer.* The captain is usually the pilot with the most seniority. He or she is in charge of the plane, with the copilot being second in command. The

103

WHAT DOES A PILOT DO?, CONTINUED

flight engineer makes preflight, inflight, and postflight inspections, adjustments, and minor repairs, and also monitors the plane's instruments during flight to make sure it is flying safely.

Aside from actually flying the aircraft, pilots have a variety of safety-related responsibilities. Before each flight, they must determine weather and flight conditions, ensure that sufficient fuel is on board to complete the flight safely, and verify the maintenance status of the aircraft. They also perform a system operation check to make sure that all instrumentation, controls, and electronic and mechanical systems are functioning properly. Before the plane takes off, the captain briefs other crew members, including flight attendants, about the flight specifics.

After all the preflight duties have been performed, the passengers have boarded, and the flight attendants have secured the cabin for takeoff, the captain taxis the aircraft to the designated runway. When the control tower radios clearance for takeoff, he or she taxis onto the runway and begins the takeoff. As the plane accelerates for takeoff, the captain focuses on the runway, while the copilot monitors the instrument panel. To determine the speed needed to become airborne, the pilot must factor in the altitude of the airport, outside temperature, weight of the plane, and wind direction.

Except for takeoff and landing, most of the time a large commercial jet is in the air, it is actually being flown on autopilot, a device that controls the plane's course and altitude, making adjustments to keep it on course. Planes today may even land on autopilot. This does not mean, however, that pilots can sit back and relax. They must constantly monitor the aircraft's systems and the weather. They also remain in constant communication with air

Lingo to Learn

Cockpit: *The area in front of the plane where pilots sit. Flight controls and instruments are located here.*

Flight hours: *Term used to describe the amount of flight time a pilot or potential pilot has accumulated. To obtain certain licenses, pilots need to fly a certain number of hours.*

Flight school: *Place where prospective pilots gain flight instruction, both in the air and on the ground. Flight schools can own or lease their planes.*

Instrument panel: *The area directly in front of the cockpit where instruments such as the altimeter, air speed indicator, and fuel gauge are located.*

Instrument rating: *Term used to describe advanced certificates pilots may earn for completing additional training that allows them to pilot a plane by using instruments only, as opposed to visuals, i.e., ground, landmarks, etc.*

Navigator: *The pilot responsible for plotting the plane's course in large aircraft, as well as monitoring instruments.*

Simulator: *Device used to test pilot's flight knowledge. Creates artificial flight circumstances.*

Revisiting Kitty Hawk

Today, in the skies above Kitty Hawk, North Carolina, private planes circle the once famous field where the first airplane flight took place on December 17, 1903. The entire flight was a scant 120 feet, but proved beyond a reasonable doubt that people possessed the ability to build a machine that was able to fly.

Near the site of the Wright brothers' first flight stands a museum housing some of the remnants of their illustrious achievements. The Wright brothers were actually bicycle makers. The intricate tools they used on their bicycles are displayed in the museum, showing that even the first pilots had a precision and a mechanical aptitude that has been one of the mainstays of pilot success ever since.

traffic controllers. As the plane travels, the pilots communicate with a series of radio navigation stations along the route.

When the cloud cover is low and visibility is poor, pilots must depend completely upon instrumentation. Altimeter readings tell them how high they are flying and whether they can fly safely over mountains and other obstacles. Special navigation radios give pilots information which, coupled with special maps, tell them their exact position.

As the plane nears its destination airport, the pilot radios the air traffic controller for clearance to approach. To land, the plane must be maneuvered and properly configured to make a landing on the runway. Once he or she has received clearance and positioned the plane for landing, the pilot extends the landing gear into the down position and sets engine power for the approach. After the plane touches down, the pilot taxis the plane to the ramp or gate area where the passengers deplane.

Pilots keep detailed logs of their flight hours, both for payroll purposes and to comply with Federal Aviation Administration regulations. They also follow "afterlanding and shutdown" procedures, and inform ground maintenance crews of any problems noted during the flight.

Flying for a large commercial airline carries much responsibility. The aircraft itself costs millions of dollars, and the safety and welfare of dozens of passengers are on the line each time a plane makes a flight. All commercial pilots must undergo continuous testing and evaluation to make sure their skills are in top shape. Each major airline has its own testing requirements, but most of them involve annual or semiannual testing of each pilot's ability. Flying and navigating are considered primary flying responsibilities. Secondary flying responsibilities include filing flight plans and listing flight reports for the FAA.

Charter pilots have essentially the same job that commercial pilots do, but on a smaller scale. Because they work for a much smaller organization with far fewer employees, charter pilots usually have more secondary flying responsibilities than commercial pilots. They may also be involved in such tasks as loading and unloading baggage, supervising refueling, keeping records, scheduling flights, arranging for major maintenance, and performing minor maintenance and repair work.

WHAT IS IT LIKE TO BE A PILOT?

For Mike Eckstein, being a pilot for Executive Air Services means being on call twenty-four hours a day. "No week is typical," he says. "You can work six days per week, or just three or four." There are FAA requirements that limit how many hours per week a pilot can fly, depending upon the type of license he or she holds. With Mike's charter license, he is allowed to fly up to eight hours per day, six days in a row. After this, he must have at least twenty-four hours off duty before he is allowed to fly again. These hours are the maximum amounts he can fly; in reality, one day may mean two hours of flying, and another day might mean six. Because his flying schedule varies so much, he never actually reaches the limits set by the FAA.

One of Mike's daily duties is preparing the flight schedule. He is normally scheduled for three or four days each week, remaining on call for the remainder of the week. When he is on call, he may be called at any time to make a flight. Because of this, he may fly six days in a row.

Variety is normal in Mike's job, which is what makes it interesting to him. For example, one day he might be called upon to take a group of vacationers to Florida and back. Another day, he may have to take a business traveler to Chicago for an early morning meeting. Besides cities throughout the United States, Mike has flown to locations in Canada and Mexico, as well.

A charter pilot's typical duties are not limited to flying the aircraft. Mike must also hand-load luggage, perform light checks on his aircraft, and file flight plans before he makes every flight. These flight plans take only minutes to complete. They are labeled "open" before a trip begins, and "closed" when the trip is finished. The purpose of these plans is to make sure there is a written record of each flight in case the plane is overdue and a search needs to be made.

To improve his flight skills, Mike sometimes spends time in flight simulators. These devices are built to simulate actual flight conditions in a variety of aircraft, from simple two-engine propeller planes to complex jets. Most flight schools have at least simple simulators for students and instructors to use.

HAVE I GOT WHAT IT TAKES TO BE A PILOT?

Most pilots have strong mechanical skills and very decisive personalities. It is very important for them to be able to make decisions quickly and accurately, sometimes under a great deal of pressure. Pilots must be responsible individuals, because the safety of their passengers depends upon them.

Pilots also need to be flexible in terms of their living location and their schedules. Even pilots who work for large commercial airlines often spend nights away from home in different cities, or even countries. And with the mergers and closings of some of the large airlines, further flexibility will be needed in the future. Today's commercial pilot cannot expect to spend his or her entire life flying and building up seniority with a single carrier.

For pilots like Mike, this flexibility takes the form of having to be on call twenty-four hours a day—ready to fly when a client calls. Also, since competition for flying jobs is so fierce, pilots should be willing to move around easily from job to job. It may not be unusual for a pilot to work for a charter service as a flight instructor, or for a private company as he or she accumulates flying hours and builds experience.

Besides certain personality characteristics, airline pilots are required by the FAA to meet certain physical requirements. They must be at least eighteen years old, be in good health, and have 20/20 vision with or without glasses. They must have good hearing and no physical disabilities that could impede their performance. They must also pass periodic and random drug screens.

To be a successful pilot, you should:

Have mechanical and technical aptitude

Be flexible in terms of your living location and schedule—you may be on call twenty-four hours a day

Be able to accept responsibility for the lives of others

Be decisive and able to make quick yet intelligent decisions in times of danger or stress

Be willing to continue your education and training your entire career

HOW DO I BECOME A PILOT?

EDUCATION

Mike's background and education are fairly typical for a charter pilot. "Actually," he says about his love of flying, "it's in my blood."

Mike decided to receive his flight education through a four-year school, which is an increasingly popular method of becoming a commercial pilot. Through such a school, you earn both a college degree (in something such as aeronautical engineering or airport operations) and a pilot's license almost simultaneously. This educational path has increased in popularity because "flying is becoming highly competitive," according to Mike. To advance as a pilot—particularly to flying for the large commercial airlines—a four-year degree is mandatory, although the degree need not necessarily be aviation-related.

Flying has become so competitive, in fact, that, as Mike says, the minimum 250 hours of flight time needed to qualify for a charter pilot's license does not count much toward a job in commercial airlines in today's marketplace. There are simply too many pilots who have reached this level of experience.

High School

Completing high school is a must if you are interested in becoming a pilot. You should take high school classes in mathematics, particularly algebra and geometry. Physics, shop classes, and meteorology, are also helpful. Good activities in which to participate include sports that may improve hand-eye coordination, a local ham radio club, and flight-oriented organizations such as the Future Aviation Professionals of America. Just as it is the legal driving age, sixteen is the age at which you can begin taking flying lessons, as well.

Postsecondary Training

There are two main routes to gaining flight experience: military training and civilian training. Military pilot training is a two-year program for which a college degree is normally required. The first year is spent learning flight basics, including classroom and simulator instruction, as well as officer training. The second year is spent training in a specific type of aircraft. Following completion of this training, pilots are expected to serve at least four years before they can leave the military and pursue a civilian flying career. On average, the military needs about four hundred new pilots per year.

Outside the military, there are nearly six hundred flight schools certified by the FAA. The cost of flight training, however, is one of the major drawbacks to this approach. According to Mike, a flight education may cost upward of $10,000, once classroom and air time are paid for.

All pilots who are paid to transport passengers must have a commercial pilot's license issued by the FAA. To obtain this license, pilots must have accumulated at least 250 hours of flying time, including at least 100 hours as pilot in command, 50 hours of cross-country, 10 hours of training in control of a complex (adjustable landing gear and props) aircraft, and 10 hours of instrument instruction.

Gary Holom-Bertelsen is an assistant flight instructor at Lewis University in Romeoville, Illinois. He spends his day in the copilot's seat, instructing students in the basics of flight. "Sometimes, I take one student up at a time, or sometimes several at once," he says. "After the flight, I write reports on their performance and go over the reports with them to monitor their progress."

Flying hours are placed in a logbook either by a flying instructor or by the pilots themselves. These logbooks serve as important records of the pilot-in-training's flying time. Besides accumulating flying hours, pilots must sometimes complete in-flight tests. These tests are called check rides. During check rides, the pilot's flying performance is rated by the flight instructor, and a pass or fail is given.

Mike says that quality, as well as quantity of flying hours is important. "It's important that you fly in a variety of conditions and get experience in a variety of aircraft," he says. In addition to time spent actually flying, pilots in training test their skills in flight simulators, which simulate such flying scenarios as night flying, thunderstorm flying, and landing without the use of an engine. High scores in flight simulators can translate into better job opportunities.

CERTIFICATION OR LICENSING

Licensing of all pilots is governed by the FAA. To obtain a commercial pilot's license the pilot must have completed the designated number of hours, and must pass an in-flight and a detailed written test.

Closely related to licensing is obtaining an instrument rating. Instrument ratings show that a pilot is able to fly based on reading instruments alone, without the help of visuals such as landmarks or clouds. These ratings change as pilots progress from flying single-engine to multiengine planes—all the way up through jets.

LABOR UNIONS

The Air Line Pilots Association International represents over forty-two thousand pilots at more than thirty airlines. A few airlines have their own pilot unions.

As with other unions, pilots pay scheduled dues to the union in exchange for a package of services that includes collective bargaining for wages and benefits.

WHO WILL HIRE ME?

About 60 percent of the 90,000 civilian pilot jobs in the 1990s were held by those working for the major airlines, such as United, USAir, Delta, and Continental. The remainder of the civilian pilots worked for smaller airlines, charter services, private corporations, or the government.

Pilot jobs are heavily concentrated in states like California, Texas, Georgia, Washington, Nevada, Hawaii, and Alaska. These states have a higher flying activity relative to their population. More than a third of all pilots work out of large centers like Dallas-Fort Worth, Los Angeles, San Francisco, New York, Chicago, Miami, and Atlanta. Seattle, Washington, DC, Denver, and Boston are also large hubs in which many pilots are based.

It will most likely be impossible for the newly licensed pilot to secure a job with a large airline. Most airlines require at least fifteen hundred hours of flying time, preferably in multiengine aircraft. The average new hire at regional airlines has over three thousand hours; the average new hire at the major airlines has over four thousand. Since most beginning pilots have not accumulated this many hours, they may want to start gaining experience by applying directly to charter companies, as Mike did.

Other employment possibilities for the beginning pilot include sightseeing companies, governmental agencies, private industry, and agricultural flying. Many of these smaller organizations require their pilots to have fewer hours of flying experience.

Faster than the Speed of Sound

In 1947, Bell Aircraft asked a twenty-four-year-old Air Force captain named Chuck Yeager to attempt something no one had ever done before. Bell wanted the World War II flying ace to fly one of its planes, the X-I, faster than the speed of sound.

The X-I was a one-seater with small, razor-thin wings and was known for its difficult maneuverability. Nevertheless, Yeager flew nearly seven hundred miles per hour, creating what is known as a sonic boom, and launching the era of the modern jet aircraft.

In 1997, on the fiftieth anniversary of his remarkable and historic feat, Chuck Yeager took an F-15 Eagle up into the wild blue yonder, and once again, broke the speed of sound.

WHERE CAN I GO FROM HERE?

Mike says that at some stage in his career he hopes to work for a major airline—but he adds that whether or not that happens depends largely on the market. In the meantime, he may be able to move to other charter airlines. He has also considered the possibility of opening his own flying service someday.

Advancement for pilots is typically limited to other flying jobs. A pilot might start out as a flight instructor, accumulating flying hours while he or she teaches. With a bit more experience, he or she might fly charter planes or perhaps get a job with a small air transportation company. Eventually, he or she might get a job with an airline. Competition for these jobs, however, is fierce, and only the best and most qualified pilots are considered.

Once a pilot breaks into the airline industry, advancement hinges almost completely upon seniority. The flight engineer or navigator may spend two to seven years before being promoted to cocaptain; once a cocaptain, he or she may spend anywhere from five to fifteen years before becoming captain. If a pilot moves from one airline to another, he or she must start over again at the bottom, and rebuild seniority.

WHAT ARE SOME RELATED JOBS?

The U.S. Department of Labor classifies airplane pilots under the heading, Airline Pilots and Navigators (DOT) and Air and Water Vehicle Operation: Air (GOE). Also included under these headings are test pilots, agricultural pilots, check pilots, facilities-flight-check pilots, flying instructors, helicopter pilots, navigators, flight-operations inspectors, and remotely-piloted vehicle controllers.

Related Jobs

Agricultural pilots

Check pilots

Facilities-flight-check pilots

Flight instructors

Flight-operations inspectors

Helicopter pilots

Navigators

Remotely-piloted vehicle controllers

Test pilots

WHAT ARE THE SALARY RANGES?

Salary ranges for pilots vary greatly—from $15,000 per year for beginning pilots at small airlines to upwards of $200,000 for captains of large airlines.

The highest paid of all pilots are those who work for the commercial airlines. In 1996, average earnings for airline pilots with six years of experience ranged from $28,100 to $76,800 per year, according to the Future Aviation Professionals of America. There are several factors that influence the pilot's salary level, including seniority, type of aircraft flown, experience level, and the airline he or she works for. Airline pilots also earn more for international and nighttime flights.

Agricultural pilots, test pilots, flight instructors, charter pilots, and pilots who work for smaller airlines receive lower salaries. Chief flight instructors averaged $24,700 per year, with top earnings of $72,000. Chief pilots of smaller airlines may make between $38,000 and $82,000.

WHAT ARE THE SALARY RANGES?, CONTINUED

Most pilots receive a benefits package that includes life and health insurance, retirement plans, and disability payments. Also, for the large commercial airlines, travel benefits are usually included in the employment package; pilots and their immediate families fly free on most airlines.

WHAT IS THE JOB OUTLOOK?

Employment of pilots is expected to grow about as fast as the average for all jobs through the year 2006. Although growth is expected in both airline passenger and cargo traffic—which normally would create more jobs—that growth will be offset by some other factors. One of these factors is the increasing use of computerized flight management systems on new aircraft. These computerized systems eliminate the need for flight engineers on those planes. Another factor is the trend toward using larger aircraft, which allows more passengers and more cargo per flight and ultimately reduces the number of flights flown.

Because of the high wages, travel benefits, and prestige, pilots tend to remain in the field once they have obtained a position. However, pilots who reach mandatory retirement age will leave the industry, generating several thousand job openings yearly.

If you are considering a career as a pilot, you should be aware, then, that you will face keen competition for jobs. Competition for pilots' jobs has intensified in recent years by an increase in the number of qualified, unemployed pilots. During the recent restructuring of the airline industry, many pilots lost their jobs. In addition, budgetary cutbacks by the federal government have resulted in many military pilots leaving the armed forces and seeking employment in the civilian sector.

Finally, employment of pilots rises and falls with the condition of the overall economy. During recessions, when there is a reduced demand for air travel, airlines cut back on their flights and consequently on their employees. Commercial and corporate flying, flight instruction, and testing of new aircraft also decline during recessions, causing a decreased need for pilots in those areas.

Tour Guide

SUMMARY

DEFINITION
Tour guides *lead groups of people on visits to sites of interest. Some guides lead short excursions, lasting only a few hours or a day. Other guides, sometimes called* tour managers, *lead groups of travelers on extended trips, lasting anywhere from a few days to a month.*

ALTERNATIVE JOB TITLES
Tour manager

SALARY RANGE
$20,000 to $35,000 to $75,000

EDUCATIONAL REQUIREMENTS
High school diploma

CERTIFICATION OR LICENSING
None

EMPLOYMENT OUTLOOK
Faster than the average

HIGH SCHOOL SUBJECTS
Foreign language
Geography
History
Sociology
Speech

PERSONAL INTERESTS
Entertaining/Performing
Helping people: personal service
Teaching
Travel

Lee Graham sits at the front of a tour bus that is lumbering through heavy New York traffic. Behind him and on the second level of the double-decker bus, seventy-five tourists swivel their heads to look at the sights he points out over a hand-held microphone.

"To your left is the Ed Sullivan Theater, where David Letterman performs," he says. "The Ed Sullivan Theater is named for the late *Daily News* columnist, who also hosted the famous television variety show. *The Ed Sullivan Show* is where Elvis had his first national television exposure, and also where the Beatles performed for their first American television audience."

Graham pauses for a sip of water. This is his third, and last, tour of the day. "And now we're coming into the heart of Times Square, where every year the famous New Year's Eve celebration takes place."

WHAT DOES A TOUR GUIDE DO?

Imagine traveling somewhere completely unfamiliar to you—a foreign country or a different city. You would probably have many questions: Where are the best places to eat? How do you get to your hotel? What sights should you see? If you were traveling outside North America, you might also have questions about language, customs, and the value of your money in foreign currency. Now

113

WHAT DOES A TOUR GUIDE DO?, CONTINUED

imagine being the person who has the answers to all those questions, and you will have an idea of what it is like to be a tour guide.

Tour guides escort groups of people who are traveling to different cities and countries. Essentially, their job is to make sure that their travelers have a safe and enjoyable trip by planning and overseeing every detail of the tour. Some guides take passengers on short excursions, which may last a few hours, a full day, or even overnight. For example, travelers visiting Los Angeles might take an all-day tour of Beverly Hills and Hollywood. Other guides—who are sometimes also called *tour managers*—accompany their groups on longer trips, lasting anywhere from a few days to a month. These longer trips generally involve travel to foreign locations and may include visits to several different cities or countries.

Tour guides are responsible for making all the necessary arrangements for a trip prior to departure. Depending upon the length and type of the trip, this could involve several different things. They might book airline flights, ground transportation such as buses or vans, hotel rooms, and tables at restaurants. If anyone in the tour group has special needs, such as dietary requirements or wheelchair accessibility, the guide must attend to these needs in advance.

Guides also plan the group's entertainment and make any necessary advance reservations. They may reserve tickets to plays, sporting events, or concerts. They may also contact other guides with specialized knowledge to give group tours of various locations. For example, for a group visiting Paris, the tour manager might arrange for a guided tour of the Louvre one day, and another guided tour of the famous Left Bank on another day.

Once the plans have been made and the tour begins, the guides' duties may include almost anything that makes the trip run smoothly. They must make sure that everything goes as planned, from transportation to accommodations to entertainment. They must see to it that passengers' luggage is loaded and routed to the proper place. They must either speak the local language or hire an interpreter, and they must be familiar enough with local customs and laws to ensure that no one in the group unwittingly does anything illegal or offensive. They must make sure that all members of the group stay together so as not to get lost, and that they are on time for various arrivals and departures.

In addition to merely monitoring the particulars of the trip and chaperoning group members, the tour guide is responsible for educating the group about the places they are visiting. Therefore, guides are generally very familiar with the locations they are visiting and are able to answer questions and provide a sort of entertaining and educational commentary throughout the trip.

Guides must be prepared to deal with unexpected difficulties or changes in plans. If a point of interest is closed, if a hotel has failed to reserve enough rooms, or if weather conditions delay travel, it is up to the guide to make alternative arrangements. The guide is also responsible for attending to whatever needs travelers might have. This could include anything from calling the hotel concierge for extra blankets to taking a sick traveler to the hospital. While tour group members are traveling in unfamiliar territory, they depend upon the tour guide for almost everything.

WHAT IS IT LIKE TO BE A TOUR GUIDE?

Lee Graham spends his days riding around the streets of New York in a double-decker bus, sharing his knowledge of the city with sixty-five to eighty other passengers. As a tour guide for Gray Line Tours, he makes three tours a day, each lasting between two and three hours.

For Gray Line guides, the day starts with a hotel courtesy pickup to bring passengers to the bus terminal, which is located in Times Square. When the tour is ready to begin, the guide greets the passengers and takes their tickets, ushering them on to the bus. "Then I deliver a little orientation," Lee says. "I explain to people what this particular tour does and where it's going. I also give a little safety lecture, about not standing while the bus is in motion, no smoking on the bus, et cetera."

Gray Line Tours has several different routes, covering most of Manhattan, according to Lee. "An uptown tour, for example, is everything north of Times Square up through 125th Street, which is a major thoroughfare in Harlem," he says. "The return leg of that route goes down the northern part of 5th Avenue. This is what we call Museum Mile, and is also the eastern perimeter of Central Park."

Lee rides either at the front or the back of the bus, speaking through a microphone to give passengers information about the sights they are seeing on the tour. He spends almost the entire tour talking. "My philosophy is that the tour guide's biggest enemy is dead air," he says. The information he gives on his tours is widely varied—some historical, some contemporary, some silly, some significant. "I'll tell them everything from how early in the morning they have to be in line to get in to see David Letterman taping to where Al Jolson first sang 'Mammy,' " he says.

On Gray Line tours, passengers have the option of getting off the bus at any of its several stops to explore that part of the city further. When they are ready to resume the tour, they can return to the bus stop and the next tour bus will pick them up. There are usually thirty minutes between buses on a downtown tour, and one hour on an uptown tour. Because of this "hop on/hop off" concept, some of Lee's passengers may be getting off the bus as the tour goes on, while new ones get on. When a tour ends, depositing passengers back at the terminal in Times Square, Lee has only about twenty minutes to rest his voice before the next tour begins. While Lee and a number of other guides are giving tours in English, other tour guides are giving tours in Spanish, German, Italian, and French. "We have a very large foreign tour operation," he says. "We run thirty-six tours in foreign languages every week."

HAVE I GOT WHAT IT TAKES TO BE A TOUR GUIDE?

According to Lee, to be a good tour guide, it is imperative that you genuinely enjoy talking in front of a group. "If you have heavy duty stage fright or don't enjoy being with groups of people, it's obviously the wrong profession for you." Because you sometimes encounter tour group members who are difficult or demanding, it is also important that you be a patient person who likes people.

Tour guides should also be fun-loving, says Lee, and help their group members enjoy themselves. "When you're on a tour, you don't want someone up there who acts like they're miserable," he says. "You want to see someone enjoying himself." Another important trait is the ability to deal with unforeseen difficulties. "If you hit traffic and can't be where you're supposed to be at 3:00, do you go to pieces or do you improvise? If someone gets sick on the tour, do you freak out, or do you deal with it? If you fall to pieces when things don't work out perfectly, this probably isn't the career for you."

Leadership and a take-charge attitude are also necessary in this job, where guides are relied upon to answer questions, deal with problems, and generally take care of travelers' needs. "Travelers are going to turn to you as the authority figure," Lee says, "and you need to feel okay about being in that role."

Finally, tour guides need to be willing and able to work long hours. During a tour, guides are never really off duty, and this can mean phone calls in the

To be a successful tour guide, you should:

Like people and enjoy communicating with them

Be able to cope with emergencies and unplanned events

Be in good health and physical condition

Feel comfortable being in charge of large groups of people

Have a good sense of humor and be fun-loving

middle of the night to resolve any problem a guest is having. For a tour manager, a workweek of eighty-five hours is not uncommon.

HOW DO I BECOME A TOUR GUIDE?

There is no one certain path to becoming a tour guide. Lee has a degree in history, and a background as a vehicle dispatcher in the military. However, much of his knowledge about New York is purely self-taught. "I had an English teacher in high school who gave me a copy of E. B. White's essay 'Here is New York,' " he says. "If you want to talk about starting an addiction . . . I haven't stopped reading about New York since."

EDUCATION

High School
A high school diploma is the minimum educational requirement for becoming a tour guide, although many guides do have some postsecondary training. If you hope to become a tour guide, there are several high school courses you can take that will prepare you for the position and improve your chances of finding a job. Perhaps the single most valuable class is a foreign language. Tour guides who can speak a second language fluently will be in the greatest demand.

A good tour guide should have a grasp of his or her destination's history and culture; therefore, classes in social studies, sociology, geography, and history are excellent choices. Since a knowledge of the arts is also important on many tours, courses in art history or appreciation would also be helpful. Because much of the tour guide's work is in communicating with people—and may often involve speaking to groups of travelers—classes in speech can help prepare you for this job.

In addition to taking the right preparatory classes, you may be able to gain experience finding a part-time or summer job working as a tour guide. Local historical sites or museums often use part-time workers or volunteers from the community to conduct tours.

Postsecondary Training
Although there is no formal educational requirement for becoming a tour guide, many guides do have some postsecondary training. Many two- and four-year colleges offer courses in tour management and tour guiding. Some trade and professional schools also offer tour guiding and tour management

programs, and a few large travel agencies offer classes to teach employees how to conduct tours.

Some tour guides—especially those interested in leading special interest tours—have bachelor's or master's degrees in various subjects. For example, someone with a degree in architecture might lead a group of travelers through Italy's churches. Or a guide with a degree in American history might lead a group on a tour of Civil War battlefields. If you hope to combine your interest in a particular field with a career as a tour guide, you should focus heavily on your area of interest, as well as taking supplemental classes in public speaking and travel and tourism, where available.

WHO WILL HIRE ME?

The major employers of tour guides are, naturally, tour companies. However, most of the major tour operators prefer experienced guides and are unlikely to take a chance on a beginner. Therefore, it may be wise to start on a smaller level. If you are familiar with a certain city, region, or local attraction, you might want to apply for a job giving tours of that area or site. Industrial plants, colleges and universities, chambers of commerce, museums, historic sites, zoos, and parks may all hire guides to give short, informational tours of their facilities. Once you have gained some experience in touring, you might then graduate to longer range, over-the-road tours conducted by tour companies.

To obtain a list of tour companies, you might approach a local travel agency and ask for help; they are likely to have a trade publication that lists all the major companies in the travel and tourism industry. The reference desk at your local library may also be able to help you compile such a list. Remember that the fastest growth in this field is likely to occur in inbound tourism; therefore, the majority of job openings will be in large cities and areas of heavy tourist traffic, such as Disney World or Nashville, Tennessee. In your job search, be sure to thoroughly explore these high-tourist areas. Check with travel agencies in those cities or consult yellow page listings under "tours" or "tour operators." Once you have a list of tour companies, you might send resumes and cover letters to the ones that interest you.

If you have attended a college or trade school, you may have the advantage of using your school's placement service to locate a job opening. The International Association of Tour Managers—North American Region also offers a placement service, as well as a job bank that matches tour managers with groups.

WHERE CAN I GO FROM HERE?

Most guides begin their careers working part-time on one-day tours. As they gain experience, they start to travel with experienced guides on a particular tour until they have mastered the itinerary and the necessary information and are able to lead that tour on their own. Career advancement can take the form of leading more complicated tours, or of specializing in a certain type of tour—such as tours to specific destinations or tours that focus on a particular interest. Guides who are good at their work often build up a following of repeat customers who sign up for their tours. These popular guides may then be able to move to a higher-paying tour company or, with the right combination of business skill and investment capital, open their own agencies.

Some tour guides become *travel writers,* reporting on various destinations for the many travel-oriented magazines and newspapers. Others may move into the corporate world, planning travel arrangements for company business travelers.

WHAT ARE SOME RELATED JOBS?

The U.S. Department of Labor classifies tour guides and others who lead groups of visitors on various sorts of tours under the heading, Guides. Other careers classified under this heading include hunting and fishing guides, alpine guides, establishment guides, sightseeing guides, dude wranglers, airport guides, plant tour guides, radio and television pages, and escorts. The U.S. Department of Labor also classifies tour managing as a coordinating and scheduling occupation. Also in this category are senior reservations agents, reservation clerks, automobile club travel counselors, crew schedulers, assignment clerks, and booking clerks. Motor vehicle and boat dispatchers, traffic clerks, and space schedulers are other examples of jobs in coordinating and scheduling.

Related Jobs

Booking clerks

Crew schedulers

Dude wranglers

Hunting and fishing guides

Motor vehicle and boat dispatchers

Passenger ship stewards and stewardesses

Plant tour guides

Radio and television pages

Reservation clerks

Senior reservation agents

Sightseeing guides

WHAT ARE THE SALARY RANGES?

The work of a tour guide is often seasonal—extremely busy during the peak travel times of May through October, and much slower in the off-season. Earnings can range from $9.75 to $20.00 per hour, not including tips. The 1997 U.S. News Career Guide Online lists the average salary for an entry-level inbound tour guide as $20,000. Average mid-level earnings are $35,000 and the top are $75,000, according to the Career Guide. While traveling, guides receive their meals and accommodations free, as well as a daily stipend to cover additional expenses.

Depending upon what tour operator they work for, tour guides may also receive a benefits package that includes sick and vacation time, health insurance, and profit sharing. Guides often also receive discounts from hotels, airlines, and transportation companies.

WHAT IS THE JOB OUTLOOK?

The travel and tourism industry is expanding and is expected to continue its growth through the year 2006. This expected increase is due in part to the fact that higher incomes and lower prices in airfare are allowing more individuals and families to travel. The market for package tours and special-interest tours—such as nature tours, wildlife tours, or architectural tours—is growing. This should create the need for more of these types of tours, and therefore, more tour guides.

Another form of tourism that is on the upswing is *inbound tourism*— guiding foreign visitors through famous American tourist sites. To many foreign travelers, America is a dream destination, with tourist spots such as Hollywood, New York, Disney World, Yellowstone, and other natural-, historical-, or cultural-rich areas drawing millions of foreign visitors each year. In 1997, *U.S. News & World Report* named inbound tour guides as one of its 20 Hot Career Jobs. The article reported that inbound tour guides with both cultural and foreign-language skills, especially Russian, German, and Japanese, would do the best in this growing subfield. Job opportunities in inbound tourism will likely be more plentiful than those guiding Americans in foreign locations. The best opportunities in inbound tourism are in large cities with international airports and in areas with a large amount of tourist traffic.

Even though tourism is on the rise, prospective tour guides should realize that there is intense competition in this field. Tour guide jobs, because of the obvious benefits, are highly sought after, so the beginning job seeker usually finds it difficult to break into the business. It is also important to remember that the travel and tourism industry is affected by the overall economy. When the economy is depressed, people have less money to spend and, therefore, travel less.

Travel Agent

> SUMMARY

DEFINITION
Travel agents *help clients make arrangements for both business and leisure travel. They make reservations for air travel, car rental, hotel accommodations, cruises, and packaged tours. To obtain fares, schedules, and availability, travel agents consult a variety of sources, such as on-line computer reservation systems, guidebooks, and other published materials.*

SALARY RANGE
$16,400 to $26,300 to $32,600

EDUCATIONAL REQUIREMENTS
High school diploma

CERTIFICATION OR LICENSING
Recommended

EMPLOYMENT OUTLOOK
Faster than the average

HIGH SCHOOL SUBJECTS
Business
Computer science
Geography/Social studies

PERSONAL INTERESTS
Computers
Helping people: personal service
Travel

It is the third week of November, and Lori Jean's phone is ringing off the hook. It seems as if everyone in town is trying to make flight reservations to get somewhere for the Christmas holiday. Unfortunately, many of the outbound flights for that week are already booked solid.

"Can you hold a moment for me?" she asks the college student on line one who wants to go home to Boise, Idaho, for Christmas. Pressing the lighted button that indicates a call on line three, she answers "All Ways Travel, Lori speaking."

"Yes, hello. I need to check pricing and availability for a round-trip flight from Chicago to San Diego for the week-end before Christmas," says the female voice on the line.

"I'd be happy to help you with that, if you can hold for just a moment, ma'am," Lori says, scrolling through her computer listing of available flights to Boise. She presses the hold button and clicks back over to the Idaho-bound college student. "Steven, I'm not showing any openings on flights for the thirteenth, but I can get you on a United flight departing at 7:10 AM on the fourteenth."

"Hmmmmm. That might work, but listen . . . can you do me a favor?" Steven says. "Can you check for the twelfth instead, maybe real late at night?"

WHAT DOES A TRAVEL AGENT DO?

Travel agents help clients make travel plans both for business and for pleasure. They serve as salespeople and consultants to their clients, providing them with information, guiding them through a decision-making process, and selling them the travel product that they decide upon. Agents may make reservations for their clients for air travel, hotel accommodations, rental cars, cruises, package tours, and rail travel.

Lingo to Learn

Airline Reporting Corporation (ARC): *An autonomous corporation created by the domestic airlines that appoints travel agencies to sell airline tickets and oversees the financial details of tracking payments to airlines and commissions to agencies.*

Booking: *A reservation.*

Coach: *The economy class on an airline.*

Computerized Reservation System (CRS): *Any of several computer systems allowing immediate access to fares, schedules, and availability, and offering the capability of making reservations and generating tickets. The two most commonly used are Sabre and Apollo.*

Confirmation number: *An alphanumeric code used to identify and document the confirmation of a booking.*

Fam: *Abbreviation for "familiarization" trip or tour. A low-cost trip or tour offered to travel agents by a supplier or group of suppliers to familiarize the agents with their destination and services.*

Layover: *A stop on a trip, usually associated with a change of planes or other transportation.*

Luxury class: *The most expensive accommodations or fare category.*

Satellite ticket printer: *A ticket printer that generates airline tickets in an ARC-accredited travel agency.*

Agents first determine their clients' needs, interests, time constraints, and budgets. Arranging leisure travel may be quite different from arranging business travel. Clients planning a vacation may want to spend considerable time in planning, learning about their different options, and looking at brochures and travel videos. Business travelers, on the other hand, often have very specific, already established requirements for travel, and want the arrangements made quickly. Whichever the type of travel, agents work with the client to design a trip that meets his or her specifications. They consult a variety of sources, such as published materials and on-line computer reservation systems, for airline departure and arrival times, fares and availability, hotel and car rental rates, and cruise and tour packages. They present information to the client and offer a choice of travel plans in an easy-to-understand fashion.

Once the client has made a decision, the agent must make the necessary reservations, issue tickets or confirmation numbers, and, in some cases, collect payment. Making reservations may be done via an on-line reservation system or via telephone. Most bookings for airlines, hotels, and rental car companies are made electronically, through a computer reservation system. To book electronically, the agent enters the client's information into the computer system, which sends it to the appropriate travel supplier. The supplier—whether it be an airline, hotel, or car rental company—reserves a seat, a room, or a car for that client. In the case of air travel reservations, the travel agent prints out an actual airline ticket on an on-site ticket printer. For hotel and car reservations, the agent receives only a confirmation number, which is printed out and passed on to the client. Tour packages and cruises are typically reserved over the telephone rather than electronically.

Travel agents may also serve as *travel consultants*. They explain about customs regulations, passports and visas, health permits, and foreign currency exchange rates. They may advise travelers on what kind of clothing to pack, baggage and accident insurance, traveler's checks, sightseeing, and restaurants.

Agents often sell package tours that are developed by another organization. In some cases, however, a group of people may ask an agent to design a tour for them. In this case, the agent sets the itinerary and makes all the necessary reservations for transportation, accommodations, meals, and activities. In addition, the agent might be responsible for providing a tour guide and publicizing the tour through brochures and advertisements.

Agents serve as bookkeepers to handle the complex details of all the trips they schedule. They serve as the go-between for the client and the supplier, making sure that arrangements are made and understood properly. They provide detailed itineraries, confirmation numbers, and tickets to their clients. In many cases, such as with air travel and cruises, they obtain payment from the client and route it to the appropriate vendor.

Travel agents may also promote their services by giving talks at social, community, or club meetings, or by suggesting company-sponsored trips to business groups. In a small agency, one or two agents may do all the sales, bookkeeping, promotion, and clerical work. In a larger agency, however, there may be clerks and secretaries who help with the clerical aspects of the job, such as filing, answering phones, and opening mail.

Although many travel agents deal with all kinds of clients and all kinds of travel, in some cases, they may specialize in either a particular kind of travel or a particular destination. Some agents may deal primarily in business travel, for example. Others may work principally with group tours or with European destinations.

WHAT IS IT LIKE TO BE A TRAVEL AGENT?

Lori Jean has been a travel agent for eight years, working for three different travel agencies in her hometown. She made the decision to pursue a career in travel and tourism while she was still in high school, and attended travel school immediately after graduation. Now, eight years later, she is still convinced that she made the right decision. "I can't think of anything else I'd rather do," she says, smiling.

The office she works in employs three agents, in addition to the agency manager. Each agent has his or her own desk and computer terminal, but they do not have individual offices. The agency is open during standard business hours—8:30 AM to 5:00 PM, Monday through Friday. None of the agents works weekends.

Most of the travel arrangements Lori makes are for air travel, both domestic and international. "Airline tickets are probably 90 percent of what I do," she says. "The rest of it is cruises and packages, either hotel and car or air and car." While some clients come into the travel agency to make their travel arrangements, most of them choose to do so over the telephone, Lori explains.

When clients call or come into the office, the first thing Lori must do is determine where, when, and how they want to travel. Some clients have much more specific desires and needs than others. For example, a client traveling on business may need a flight that gets him or her to the destination by a certain time, while a client traveling for pleasure can choose from several flight times and options.

Once she has obtained the passenger information, Lori puts the information into her computer's reservation system. "If I'm checking availability for an airline, hotel, or car, I can just put in their information, their travel dates and what they want, and my computer pulls up everything available, starting with the lowest price," she says. If she is making both air travel and land arrangements—a rental car or hotel room—for her clients, she always checks and confirms the air travel first. This way, she knows exactly what time her clients will be arriving at their destination and what time they will need their cars and accommodations.

After the client has decided on a flight, hotel, or car, Lori makes the reservations. "To make reservations, I have to get the names of the people who will be traveling and their addresses and telephone numbers," Lori says. "It's very important when getting names that the name on the ticket exactly matches the name that's on the client's driver's license. For example, if the driver's license said William and the ticket said Bill, the airlines would have the right not to let that person board because of the discrepancy." Lori enters all passenger information into her computer's reservation system, which sends it directly to the airline, car rental company, or hotel.

Lori also asks clients how they wish to pay. If they are reserving an airline ticket or a cruise, they pay Lori's travel agency; for cars and hotels, however, they pay the hotel or car rental company directly when they check in. Lori says that when clients buy airline tickets, it is her agency's policy that they must pay before the tickets are printed. "Many people pay with credit cards," she says, "so in that case, they can pay right then over the phone and I can print the ticket for them." Other times, clients come into the office to pay for their tickets.

Some airline tickets have restrictions, meaning that they are nonrefundable and the airline charges a penalty for changing the flight time. If there are any restrictions on the ticket that her client is purchasing, Lori must inform him or her of those restrictions.

Once the client has given Lori all the necessary information and has been informed of any restrictions on the ticket, the next step is to print the ticket. Like most travel agencies, Lori's office has an airline ticket printer on-site. "To generate a ticket, it's just a matter of making an entry into the system and having it print out," she says. If she is reserving a car or a hotel room, Lori gives her client a confirmation number rather than a ticket. The confirmation number is generated by the hotel or car rental company, and ensures that the hotel or car is, in fact, being held for her client.

Booking a passenger on a cruise is slightly different. There is a lot more information to get from passengers booking a cruise," Lori says. "They have a lot more choices." For some cruise bookings, she must check to make sure that her clients have a passport and/or proof of citizenship. She must also ask passengers their preferences on dining-room sittings, special diets, cabin size, and whether they need smoking or nonsmoking areas."

Once she has obtained all the necessary information, she books the cruise directly with the cruise line reservation agent. "With a cruise, everything is done over the phone and we don't generate any of the documentation," she says. "The cruise line prints up the documents and mails them to our office. When they come in, we check them for correctness and pass them on to the clients."

HAVE I GOT WHAT IT TAKES TO BE A TRAVEL AGENT?

Lori says the key requirement for being a good travel agent is the ability to communicate. "You can always learn how to operate the computer, and anyone can be trained to call a cruise line and book a trip," she says, "but you really have to be able to get along with the client, know what to ask them, how to make them feel comfortable." She says that if an agent doesn't communicate well with the client, the client may not trust that agent to make the right arrangements and get the best deal.

> **❝You can always learn how to operate the computer . . . but you really have to be able to get along with the client, know what to ask them, how to make them feel comfortable.❞**

Some selling skills are also important, according to Lori. "You don't have to be a high-powered sales person, but you do need to have some assertiveness in that area," she says. "If a person is waffling, you need to be able to push them a little."

Patience and a tolerance for stress are also necessary to success in this field. During peak travel times, such as holidays and spring break, the travel agent's job can become very stressful. "In really busy times, it gets frustrating, because you have people calling and there's nothing you can do for them," Lori says. "It gets to the point where you search every single flight for the days they want and still can't find availability. That's frustrating for both you and them."

To be a successful travel agent, you should:

Have excellent communication skills

Be enthusiastic, patient, and courteous in dealing with people

Have some sales ability

Have an interest in travel

Be precise and detail-oriented in your work habits

Be able to concentrate on your work despite interruptions and a lack of privacy

The best part of the job for Lori is the opportunity to learn about new places. "What I really like is that I get to find out about places that before I'd never heard of and places I will probably never visit," she says. She also enjoys the chance to help people make their travel plans. "I really like being able to plan someone's dream vacation or their honeymoon," she says. "When someone comes in and they've saved for years and they've always wanted to go to Hawaii, just to be able to do that for them is a big plus."

Yet another benefit of the job is that it allows her to travel at a much reduced cost. "All airlines offer special agent fares, which are substantially reduced from full coach fare," she says, "and most hotels and car companies also offer some type of special price for travel agents."

How Do I Become a Travel Agent?

EDUCATION

High School

A high school diploma is the minimum requirement for becoming a travel agent. If you are interested in pursuing a career as an agent, be certain to include some computer courses, as well as typing or keyboarding courses, in your class schedule. Since much of your work as a travel agent will involve computerized reservation systems, it is important to have basic keyboarding skills and to be comfortable working with computers.

Because being able to communicate clearly with clients is central to this job, any high school course that enhances communication skills, such as English or speech, is a good choice. Proficiency in a foreign language, while not a requirement, might be helpful in many cases, such as when you are working with international travelers. Finally, geography, social studies, and business mathematics are classes that may also help prepare you for various aspects of the travel agent's work.

You can also begin learning about being a travel agent while still in high school by getting a summer or part-time job in travel and tourism. D. G. Elmore, president of Gant Travel—a national chain of corporate travel agencies—suggests that interested high school students find a job in a travel agency, doing whatever they can do. "I would advise them to get a job doing anything from tearing down tickets to delivering tickets. Anything that brings them in contact with the business will go a long way toward getting them a job," he says. "If they did that their senior year in high school in a major city, they'd have a job by the end of the summer, almost certainly." If finding a part-time or summer job in a travel agency proves impossible, you might consider looking for a job as a reservation agent for an airline, rental car agency, or hotel.

Postsecondary Training

Currently, most travel agencies do not require their agents to have college degrees. Some college background may be helpful, however; when it comes to advancement, the agent with more education is likely to have an edge over those with less. Some colleges offer two- and four-year degrees in travel and tourism. If your college of choice does not offer a specific degree in travel and tourism, a degree in geography, communication, business, or foreign languages might be equally helpful. Other good college courses to take include computer science, world history, and accounting.

Another option for prospective travel agents is to take a short-term course in travel specifically designed to prepare you for work in this field. Such courses are typically between six and eighteen weeks in length and are offered by community colleges, vocational schools, and adult education programs. The American Society of Travel Agents (ASTA) offers a correspondence course that provides a basic understanding of the industry, and there are a number of travel schools that combine home study with on-site training to prepare future agents.

In the Know: Books and Magazines for Travel Professionals

Books

Your Career in Travel and Tourism, *Merton House Publishing Company*

The Travel Agent: Dealer in Dreams, *Kendal/Hunt Publishing Company*

So . . . You Want to Be a Travel Agent, *Prentice Hall*

Travel Agent, *Arco Publishing*

Magazines

Business Travel News

Conde Nast

Travel Age

Travel Agent Magazine

Traveler

Travel News

Travel Weekly

Lori trained at such a travel school, completing a number of lessons through a home-study course and then spending six weeks taking classes at the actual school. "During the classes, we covered two basic modules," she says. "In the mornings, we learned about reservations, how to interact with the client, what to ask, and went over information on airlines, hotels, and cruises. In the afternoons, we covered ticketing, how to work with computer systems, how to pull up and enter all the information to book a ticket."

CERTIFICATION

Most states do not require travel agents to be licensed or registered. However, there are exceptions, so it is important to check the requirements for the state in which you will be working.

Travel agents may choose to become certified by the Institute of Certified Travel Agents (ICTA). ICTA offers certification programs leading to the designations of "Certified Travel Associate" (CTA) and "Certified Travel Counselor" (CTC). In order to become a Certified Travel Associate, agents must have eighteen months of experience as a travel agent, complete a twelve-course program, and pass a written test. In order to become a Certified Travel Counselor, agents must have five years of experience, must have attained their CTA status, must take a twelve-course program, and take and pass a final exam. While not a requirement, certification by ICTA may help an agent progress in his or her career.

ICTA also offers travel agents a number of other programs such as sales skills development courses, and destination specialist courses, which provide a detailed knowledge of various geographic regions of the world.

WHO WILL HIRE ME?

Lori says that it was not difficult to find her first job as a travel agent. "I sent out resumes to several agencies, and got called in for interviews," she says. "I think after I put my resumes out, it was maybe a month to two months before I actually started my job. It's usually not a hard industry to get into."

There are approximately 140,000 travel agents currently working in the United States. Agents may work for commercial travel agents, in the corporate travel department of a large company, or be self-employed. Most agents work for travel agencies; approximately only 10 percent are self-employed.

Most new travel agents find jobs by applying directly to travel agencies. The job seeker might pinpoint a geographic area he or she is interested in and send resumes and cover letters to all the agencies in that area. Job openings for travel agents are also sometimes listed in the classified section of local newspapers, travel magazines, and industry publications. ASTA's publication, *Travel News,* includes a classified section that lists job opportunities for agents.

If the agent has recently graduated from a travel school, he or she may get formal or informal placement assistance through that school. Some schools, for example, announce their graduating classes in industry publications and arrange interviews with potential employers. Others maintain a listing of job openings for their students' use.

WHERE CAN I GO FROM HERE?

Lori says she enjoys being a travel agent so much that she is content to stay where she is. "I'm happy doing what I do, and I would be happy just to remain your average travel agent," she says. "The only other step for me is to move up to *office manager* or *agency manager,* which involves more administrative work that really has nothing to do with travel."

Advancement opportunities for travel agents are, as Lori points out, somewhat limited. Experienced and skilled agents may advance to the position of office or agency manager. These managers are usually responsible for overseeing other travel agents, generating various reports, keeping track of finances, and generally managing all the activities of the travel agency.

The travel agent with capital, business skills, and a good following of clients might eventually open his or her own travel agency. In order to do this, he or she must generally have approval from supplier organizations, such as the Airlines Reporting Corporation and the International Travel Agency Network.

In addition to jobs in the regular travel business, a number of travel jobs are available with oil companies, automobile clubs, and transportation companies. Some state and local governments also hire travel professionals for their departments of tourism. Agents with several years of experience may be eligible for a job with one of these organizations.

WHAT ARE SOME RELATED JOBS?

The U.S. Department of Labor classifies travel agents under the heading, Sales Occupations, Transportation Services (DOT). Other occupations listed under this heading include traffic agents, crating-and-moving estimators, and sales representatives (shipping services).

Related Jobs

Airline reservation agents

Crating-and-moving estimators

Hotel concierges

Rental car agents

Sales representatives (shipping services)

Tour guides

Traffic agents

There are several jobs within the travel and tourism industry that are similar to the travel agent's. Airlines, car rental companies, tour packaging operators, cruise lines, and hotels and motels frequently employ their own reservation agents who perform duties much like those performed by travel agents. The work of *hotel concierges*—who offer advice on restaurants, shows, museums, and tours, and sometimes also make travel arrangement for hotel patrons—is similar in certain ways to the work of travel agents. *Tour guides,* who lead tour groups on visits to cultural, historical, and natural landmarks, also occasionally perform duties that are similar to those of the travel agent.

WHAT ARE THE SALARY RANGES?

Travel agency income comes from commissions paid by airlines, hotels, car rental companies, cruise lines, and tour operators. Although many suppliers pay a standard 8 percent—recently reduced from 10 percent (see sidebar)—of the total cost to the customer, commissions do vary somewhat. Cruise lines, for example, pay commissions on a sliding scale depending upon the season.

Fees-for-Service: A New Travel Agency Trend

The next time you or your parents contact a travel agent to make reservations for a flight or cruise to Hawaii or to Europe or even to see Aunt Madge in Duluth by train or bus, don't be surprised if you are charged a fee for this service.

You've already learned how income for travel agencies comes from commissions paid by airlines, and other leisure-service entities. On September 18, 1997, United Airlines reduced its travel agents' commission from 10 percent to 8 percent. In the following months more than 20 other airlines followed suit, ruffling the feathers of travel agents who depend on these commissions for their livelihood. In 1996, nearly $65 billion worth of tickets were issued by travel agencies—that's over 80 percent of all airline tickets sold.

In response to this cut in commission, some travel agencies now impose flat fees regardless of the type and expense of trip a customer books; others have resisted passing the buck on to their customers.

A recent survey by the Public Interest Research Group reported that travel agents—not airlines—still locate the lowest fares for consumers. But expect these low fares to come at a price. The old adage is true—nothing in life is ever free.

Travel agents typically earn a straight salary. Although less common, some agents are paid a salary plus commission or entirely on a commission basis. According to a Louis Harris survey, an average entry-level salary in 1996 for a travel agent was $16,400 per year. Agents with five years or more experience might expect to earn from $26,300 to $32,600. In addition to experience level, the location of the firm is also a factor in how much travel agents earn. Agents working in larger metropolitan areas tend to earn more than their counterparts in smaller cities.

One of the benefits of working as a travel agent is the chance to travel at a discounted price. Major airlines offer special agent fares, which are often only 25 percent of regular cost. Hotels, car rental companies, cruise lines, and tour operators also offer reduced rates for travel agents. Agents also get the opportunity to take free or low-cost group tours sponsored by transportation carriers, tour operators, and cruise lines. These trips, called "fam" trips, are designed to familiarize agents with locations and accommodations so that they can better market them to their clients.

In addition to travel benefits, most agents also receive a standard benefits package that includes medical insurance and paid holidays, sick days, and vacations. The quality of the benefits package may depend upon the size of the agency, however; some smaller agencies provide less-than-average benefits for their employees.

WHAT IS THE JOB OUTLOOK?

The employment outlook for travel agents is good. The travel and tourism industry, as a whole, is growing significantly. Spending on travel—both business-related and leisure—is expected to increase substantially in the next ten years. Americans are finding it easier to travel than ever before for a number of reasons. Rising household incomes, smaller families, and early retirements have all made leisure travel more feasible for many individuals. In addition, more efficient airplanes and competition within the airline industry have lowered the cost of air travel, bringing it within the budgets of more people. Finally, a growing number of foreign visitors to the United States is expected to boost overall industry sales.

There are some factors, however, that may negatively influence the growth of jobs for travel agents. Many airlines and other travel suppliers now offer consumers the option of making their own travel arrangements through on-line reservation services, readily accessible through the Internet. With this as an option, it is possible that travelers will become less dependent upon agents to make travel arrangements for them. In addition, airlines have placed a limit on the amount of commission they will pay travel agencies. This could potentially reduce an agency's income, thereby making it less profitable and less able to hire new travel agents. The impact of these practices, however, has yet to be determined.

While currently thriving, the travel industry is sensitive to economic changes and political crises that may cause international travel plans to be postponed. Therefore, the number of job opportunities for agents may fluctuate, depending upon the general political and economic climate.

What
Can I Do
Right
Now?

travel & hospitality

Get Involved: A Directory of Camps, Programs, Competitions, Etc.

FIRST

Now that you've read about some of the different careers available in hospitality and travel, you may be anxious to experience this line of work for yourself, to find out what it's *really* like. Or perhaps you already feel certain that this is the career path for you and want to get started on it right away. Whichever is the case, this section is for you! There are plenty of things you can do right now to learn about hospitality and travel careers while gaining valuable experience. Just as important, you'll get to meet new friends and see new places, too.

In the following pages, we list many specific programs around the USA that make the hospitality and travel industry accessible, in some measure, to high school students. Your opportunities range from flying with an experienced pilot to studying for a certificate in the management of lodgings. Some will keep you busy during the school year, others will fill up your summer vacations. We've categorized all of the programs in this book for your convenience; it's up to you to decide whether you're interested in one particular type of program or are open to a number of possibilities. The categories into which programs fall are listed right after the name of the program or organization, so you can skim through to find the listings that interest you most.

THE CATEGORIES

Camps
We list only one camp in this book but you may be able to find more, especially if you are interested in adventure tourism and other careers that lend themselves to this kind of program. If you are hunting for camps, bear in mind that certain academic programs bill themselves as camps—computer camps, science camps, et cetera—but often have little to do with the outdoors.

Employment Opportunities
The hospitality and travel industry offers plenty of opportunities for young people looking for their first jobs. Many, if not most, hotels and related establishments have some kind of entry-level position open to high school students. (Airlines are, of necessity, a different matter.) We list several such employment opportunities in this book—including a number at theme and amusement parks—and you should have little trouble locating others in your area.

Internships
Basically, an internship combines the responsibilities of a job (strict schedules, pressing duties, and usually written evaluations by your supervisor) with the uncertainties of a volunteer position (no wages or fringe benefits, no guarantee of future employment). That may not sound very enticing, but completing an internship is a great way to prove your maturity, your commitment to the hospitality and travel industry, and your knowledge and skills to colleges, potential employers, and yourself. Some internships here are just formalized volunteer positions, others offer unique responsibilities and opportunities: choose the kind that works best for you!

Memberships
When an organization is in this category, it simply means that you are welcome to pay your dues and become a card-carrying member. Formally joining any organization has the benefits of meeting others who share your interests and concerns, finding opportunities to take action, and keeping up with current events in the field and in the group. Depending on how active you are, the contacts you make and experiences you gain may help when the time comes to apply to colleges or look for a job.

In some organizations, you may pay a special student rate but receive virtually the same benefits as a regular adult member. Most groups have student branches with special activities and publications. Don't let membership dues discourage you from contacting any of these organizations. Most charge only a nominal fee because they know that students are perpetually short of funds. If the fees are still too much for your budget, contact the group that interests you anyway—they are likely to at least send you some information and place you on their mailing list.

Study and Training

There are a number of different ways to formally train for a career in hospitality and travel. A college degree—associate's or bachelor's—is one way, and you can also study at trade schools or even through correspondence courses. This book offers ways to start pursuing each of these methods of preparation. It is important to explore more than one option and to make sure that the training you receive really will help you land the job you want. Before you commit yourself to a training program or course of study, seek advice from your guidance counselor and even from the human resources departments of companies for which you might like to work.

Volunteer Opportunities

Generally speaking, the volunteer opportunities you'll find in this book and around the hospitality and travel industry amount to informal internships. As a volunteer, you can expect to work fewer hours and receive less training than an intern—which gives you more flexibility while requiring less commitment from you. This makes volunteering a particularly good option if you just want to explore potential career paths instead of seriously starting out on one. Having said that, it is nevertheless true that volunteering can mark the beginning of your career if you want it to.

PROGRAM DESCRIPTIONS

Once you've started to look at the individual listings themselves, you'll find that they contain a lot of information. Naturally, there is a general description of the program(s), but wherever possible we also have included the following details.

Application Information

Each listing notes how far in advance you'll need to apply for the program or position, but the simple rule is to apply as far in advance as possible. This ensures that you won't miss out on a great opportunity simply because other people got there ahead of you. It also means that you will get a timely decision on your application, so if you are not accepted, you'll still have some time to apply elsewhere. As for the things that make up your application, such as essays and recommendations—we've tried to tell you what's involved, but be sure to contact the program about specific requirements before you submit anything.

Background Information

This includes such information as the date the program was established, the name of the organization that is sponsoring it financially, and the faculty and staff who will be there for you. This can help you—and your family—gauge the quality and reliability of the program.

Classes and Activities

Classes and activities offered through the programs listed here may change over time or be listed under different names. Thus, when we list specific course titles or activities, they are offered as more of a general guide than a fixed curriculum. Still, you can be fairly confident that travel schools will offer courses in ticketing and reservations and that theme parks will offer free rides to their employees on their days off—such things are simply standard practice.

Contact Information

Wherever possible, we have given the *title* of the person whom you should contact instead of the *name* because people change jobs so frequently. If no title is given and you are telephoning an organization, simply tell the person who answers the phone the name of the program or position that interests you and he or she will forward your call. If you are writing, include the line "Attention: Summer Study Program" (or whatever is appropriate after "Attention") somewhere on the envelope. This will help to ensure that your letter goes to the person in charge of that program.

Credit

Where some programs and opportunities are concerned, we sometimes note that high school or college credit is available to those who have completed them. This means that the program can count toward your high school diploma or a future college degree just like a regular course. Obviously, this can be very useful, but it's important to note that rules about accepting such credit vary from school to school and college to college. Before you commit to a program offering high school credit, check with your guidance counselor to see if it is acceptable at your school. As for programs offering college credit, check with your chosen college (if you have one) to see if they will accept it.

Eligibility and Qualifications

In each listing, we try to include the minimum requirements for participation. Beyond that, we mention other requirements when specified by the sponsoring organizations and employers, but these vary widely and may even change as their programs and job openings evolve. Some require recommendations, certain GPAs or other academic achievements, or personal statements and interviews. Be sure you understand all of the current eligibility requirements before you apply.

Facilities

We try to include information on such facilities as accommodations, computer equipment, and the like. This is something to pay attention to as you gather more information about the programs that interest you, because the quality of the facilities can really affect your enjoyment of the programs.

Financial Details

You and your family should consider your financial situation before deciding whether you need to earn money or can afford to volunteer or pay to participate in a program. It's true that any money you put into career exploration and training is an investment in your future, but you have to be practical about these things. If you really want to pursue a training or study course but face financial difficulties, look into financial aid or payment plan options before giving up on the idea.

Residential vs. Commuter Options

Simply put, some programs prefer that participating students live with other participants and staff members, others do not, and still others leave the decision entirely to the students themselves. As a rule, residential programs are suitable for young people who live out of town or even out of state, as well as for local residents. Commuter programs may be viable only if you live near the program site or if you can stay with relatives who do. Bear in mind that for residential programs especially, the travel between your home and the location of the activity is almost always your responsibility and can significantly increase the cost of participation.

FINALLY . . .

Ultimately, there are three important things to bear in mind concerning all of the programs listed in this volume. The first is that things change. Staff members come and go, funding is added or withdrawn, supply and demand determine which programs continue and which terminate. Dates, times, and costs vary widely because of a number of factors. Because of this, the information we give you, although as current and detailed as possible, is just not enough on which to base your final decision. If you are interested in a program, you simply must write, call, fax, or email the organization in charge to get the latest and most complete information available. This has the added benefit of putting you in touch with someone who can deal with your individual questions and problems.

You should also note that the editors of this book cannot actually recommend or endorse any particular programs or organizations. Use the contact information we give you to explore the quality and suitability of the opportunities listed and to determine what is right for you.

The other third thing to bear in mind is that the programs listed here are just the tip of the iceberg. No book can possibly cover all of the opportunities that are available to you—partly because they are so numerous and are constantly coming and going, but partly because some are waiting to be discovered. For instance, you may be very interested in volunteering for a tourist board but don't see a listing for one in your area. Why not just go to your local tourist authority, explain your interest in career exploration, and volunteer your services? They may already have a program for you to join or they may start one because you were the first person to show an interest. Or perhaps you would like to take a training course but don't see the school that interests you in the listings. Call their Admissions Office! Even if they don't have a special program for high school students, they should be able to arrange for you to at least visit and sit in on a class. Use the ideas behind these listings and take the initiative to turn them into opportunities!

THE PROGRAMS

AVIATION INFORMATION RESOURCES, INC.

Study/Training

The organization Aviation Information Resources (AIR), the "Airline Career Specialists," is a little difficult to categorize for this book, but is definitely worth knowing. Most of AIR's members are established pilots seeking advanced or different positions, but the company also works with young people who are just beginning their aviation careers. AIR offers two publications of special interest to students: *Airline Pilot Careers: The Future Airline Pilot's Magazine* and "The Ultimate Airline Pilot Starter Kit." The magazine profiles a major airline each month and includes other feature articles and advice columns. The kit is filled with information, starting with the very basic "How to Become an Airline Pilot," moving on to more advanced concepts such as "Certificate and Rating Requirements" and "Choosing a Flight School." It also includes appendices listing "Common Training Aircraft," "Aviation Organizations," and the like. Aviation Information Resources also offers seminars and job fairs at various locations around the country throughout the year. While these may not be helpful to the absolute beginner, you may benefit from them if you already have some piloting experience. Contact AIR for more information on membership, publications, and gatherings—much of this is available on their Web site.

■ **Aviation Information Resources, Inc.**
1001 Riverdale Court
Atlanta, GA 30337-6005
Tel: 800-AIR-APPS
Web: http://www.airapps.com

BETSY ROSS TOURS

Internship

Betsy Ross Tours welcomes high school students who would like to apply for internships with the company. Founded in 1980, the company is dedicated to providing complete package tours of the Washington, DC, area to groups visiting the nation's capitol. As an intern for Betsy Ross Tours, your duties include making tour reservations with vendors around the city, typing room lists for hotels, and carrying out such general office duties as filing, answering the phones, and handling routine business correspondence. To complete these tasks, you need excellent communication skills and computer or typing experience, and must pay attention to detail and follow each project through to completion, sometimes working independently. Interns must live nearby and provide their own transportation. They must also set up and stick to a schedule. For more information about this opportunity to intern in the travel industry, contact Elizabeth Ross, the president of Betsy Ross Tours.

■ **Betsy Ross Tours**
5125 MacArthur Boulevard, NW, Suite 37
Washington, DC 20016
Tel: 202-364-1954

BIG APPLE GREETER

Volunteer Opportunity

Big Apple Greeter is a nonprofit organization whose mission is to enhance New York City's image by helping visitors discover its hidden treasures. If you live in New York and love everything about it, perhaps there's a tour guide hidden in you. Volunteer tour guides welcome visitors to all five boroughs and show them that the big city can have small-town charm. Greeters personally take visitors to neighborhoods, cultural attractions, historic sites, and hot spots that only a New Yorker would know. If you'd prefer a behind-the-scenes role, the opportunities include responding to inquiries from visitors, matching greeters with visitors, and providing general office and data-entry assistance. This is a great way to gain experience in the field of hospitality and tourism. Get all the details by phone, fax, or mail, or check out Big Apple Greeter's Web site, where you can apply for volunteer positions on-line.

Big Apple Greeter
One Centre Street, 19th Floor
New York, NY 10007
Tel: 212-669-2364 (Volunteer Info)
Web: http://www.bigapplegreeter.org

BOY SCOUTS OF AMERICA AVIATION EXPLORING

Membership

The Boy Scouts of America (BSA) invites young men and women who have completed the eighth grade to participate in its Aviation Exploring program. This program is part of a wider initiative of setting up Explorer posts around the country, with each post exploring a career field—including aviation—that is of particular interest to its members. This means that there may already be an Aviation Exploring post in your area, but if there isn't, you can help to set one up if there are enough young people interested in becoming members and adults interested in becoming advisers. Aviation Exploring posts meet regularly to consider such topics as "Learning to Fly," "Professional Pilots and Flight Engineers," and "Nonflying Aviation Careers." Much of the exploration consists of hands-on projects, visits to airports and other important sites, and visits from guest speakers who work in the field. All Explorer posts, regardless of their career focus, also make a commitment to the BSA's principles of leadership, service, social responsibility, physical and mental health, and respect for the outdoors. How this commitment is enacted varies from post to post. If you think you might be interested in joining an Aviation Exploring post, ask your guidance counselor for help in contacting or starting one, or contact the National Office of the Boy Scouts of America at the address below.

■Boy Scouts of America Aviation Exploring
1325 West Walnut Hill Lane
PO Box 152079
Irving, TX 75015-2079
Tel: 214-580-2000

CHALLENGE Program

Study/Training

High school students with a strong interest in aviation might consider taking part in the Challenge summer program at St. Vincent College. Challenge offers one week of courses for gifted, talented, and creative young people who want to explore new interests in a stimulating environment. The program, which runs in late July, generally provides courses in such areas as robotics, video production, and aviation. Participants have the option of commuting to classes daily or of living on campus and participating in evening activities. Commuters can expect to pay about $325 for the entire program, while residents pay closer to $475. Contact the Program Coordinator to check the availability of an aviation course and for further details about Challenge. There is also a separate Challenge session for middle school students held in mid-July; the Program Coordinator can provide more information.

■CHALLENGE Program
St. Vincent College
300 Fraser Purchase Road
Latrobe, PA 15650
Tel: 412-537-4569

COLLEGE AND CAREERS Program

Study/Training

The Rochester Institute of Technology (RIT) offers rising seniors the chance to explore college life while looking at careers in the hospitality field. RIT's College and Careers program is held over a Friday and Saturday twice each summer. Participants choose up to four sessions on career topics that interest them; you may be especially interested in such sessions as "Explore a Career in Food Management" and "Explore Hospitality Careers." While actual session titles may change from year to year, you can always expect hands-on learning and advice from graduates or professionals in the field. The format of the College and Careers program also allows you to pursue your interests outside of hospitality, such as technology, business, and art. Electing to spend Friday night in the RIT residence halls (as is strongly encouraged) gives you the chance to participate in social activities and meet other college-bound students. The deadlines to apply for this program are only about one week before the actual dates in July and August; however, you are advised to apply early as space is limited and is allotted on a first come, first served basis. The College and Careers program will cost you only about $45 for the seminars, meals, and accommodations, or about $30 for just the seminars and meals. Contact the Office of Admissions for details about this year's program.

■ **College and Careers Program**
Rochester Institute of Technology
Office of Admissions, 60 Lomb Memorial Drive
Rochester, NY 14623-5604
Tel: 716-475-6635

EDUCATION SYSTEMS

Study/Training

Education Systems can help you explore travel careers in two different ways. First, it offers a high school curriculum on the tourism and hospitality industry. If there is enough interest in this career area among your classmates, ask your principal to look into the possibility of using this curriculum. If you're on your own, Education Systems' other offering is a complete correspondence course on becoming a travel agent. Consisting of six separate study sections and software that simulates the most widely used computer reservation systems, the course costs $825. That price includes the grading of your exams (all of which must be sent to Education Systems), certificates of completion for each section and the course as a whole, and contact with a personal tutor. The course must be completed one year from the starting date, but you should be able to finish in three months if you apply yourself. You also have the option of studying only individual sections of the course, including "Fares and Tickets" and "Geography of the Western Hemisphere," for $125 each. These options represent major investments of time and money, so you need to be pretty confident of your career choice before committing to them. Education Systems will provide you with all the details you need to make a decision.

■ **Education Systems**
11038 Longdale Circle
Sandy, UT 84092
Tel: 800-288-3987
Web: http://www.educationsystems.com
Email: travel@educationsystems.com

EDUCATIONAL INSTITUTE OF THE AMERICAN HOTEL AND MOTEL ASSOCIATION

Study/Training

The American Hotel and Motel Association (AHMA) is a major player in the hospitality and travel industry. Its Educational Institute administers distance-learning courses for professionals wanting to advance within the industry and, more importantly for you, for those just starting out. You can take single courses to give yourself an edge in the job market ("Introduction to the Hospitality Industry" would seem to be ideal) or take a specified number to earn a certification (perhaps you'd like to be a Certified Lodging Manager or something of that sort). AHMA's Educational Institute says that its courses are comparable to those you would take at a college, so this may be an option worth pursuing. A single course costs about $175, and you have four months to complete it. Contact the Educational Institute of the American Hotel and Motel Association for information on its current course offerings and all the other details you need.

 ■ **Educational Institute of the American Hotel and Motel Association**
   1407 South Harrison Road, Suite 300
   East Lansing, MI 48823-5239
   Tel: 800-344-3320 or 517-353-5500
   Web: http://www.ei-ahma.org

EURAM FLIGHT CENTRE

Employment Opportunity

EurAm (a condensation of "European American") Flight Centre is a travel agency that often has employment opportunities for high school students interested in the tourism industry. One of the most common positions available to young people is that of Reservation Sales Agent. In this job, you "create and maintain reservations through telephone sales." Applicants for this position must type at least twenty-five words per minute, have a working knowledge of national and international geography, and be able to clearly communicate with customers over the telephone. There is generally a paid training period before you begin working for an hourly rate (presently about $8) plus commission. Other positions at EurAm are also frequently available to high school students, with varying requirements and rates of pay. For more information, contact Human Resources at the Euram Flight Centre.

 ■ **EurAm Flight Centre**
   1522 K Street, NW
   Washington, DC 20005
   Tel: 202-789-2255

EXPERIMENTAL AIRCRAFT ASSOCIATION

Membership

The Experimental Aircraft Association (EAA) is eager to get young people interested and involved in its aviation activities. Its Young Eagles Flight Program matches young people fascinated by flight with adult pilots eager to share their enthusiasm for aviation. Young Eagles actually fly with their pilots. EAA Project Schoolflight gets students working on aircraft design and construction right in their own schools. There are many other programs—including camps, scholarships, and academies—you can take part in by becoming a member of the Experimental Aircraft Association. The cost of a young adult membership (for those ages eighteen and under) is about $20 and includes a subscription to *Sport Aviation* magazine. Contact the EAA for details.

> **Experimental Aircraft Association**
> PO Box 3065
> Oshkosh, WI 54903-3065
> Tel: 414-426-4800
> Fax: 414-426-6560
> Web: http://www.eaa.org

FLIGHT TRAINING ADVENTURE CAMP

Camp

If you're ready to move toward becoming a pilot, this program can get you going. Flight Training Adventures offers three-week camps that encompass adventures like river rafting, water skiing, spelunking, horseback riding, hiking, primitive camping, parachuting, swimming, cliff jumping, bicycling—and, yes, flight training. These camps are for young people between the ages of fifteen and twenty. Campers who plan to make their first solo flight must be at least sixteen years old, and those who plan to obtain their private pilot's license must be at least seventeen. Flight Training Adventure Camp offers a complete brochure on-line describing the philosophy behind these camps. Detailed information about the camp's costs can be found by clicking on the Calendar & Rates page. To get the best descriptions of the camp, read through the sections called Member Reports and Endorsements/Testimonials, or phone, fax, email, or write for details.

> **Flight Training Adventure Camp**
> PO Box 1971
> Fairfield, IA 52556
> Tel: 515-472-5217
> Web: http://www.ftacamp.com
> Email: ftac@fairfield.net

HERSHEYPARK
Employment Opportunity

Hersheypark is a theme park based in Hershey, Pennsylvania—home of a certain chocolate empire. It offers high school students the chance to gain experience in the tourism industry by working at any one of a number of jobs. Positions available each year include those in entertainment, food service, games, guest services, merchandise and sales, and operations. In addition to your basic paycheck, as a Hersheypark employee you receive free admission during non-work hours, free guest passes, and admission arrangements to several other theme parks. If your performance is satisfactory, Hersheypark also provides you with a letter of recommendation. The park is open from April to September, but the Employment Office is open from March through August. Contact the Employment Office early for the best openings and for full details about working at Hersheypark.

Hersheypark
100 West Hersheypark Drive
Hershey, PA 17033
Tel: 717-534-3326

INTERN EXCHANGE INTERNATIONAL, LTD.
Internship

Since 1987, Intern Exchange International has combined summertime internships at top-flight businesses with travel to London, England. High school students ages sixteen to eighteen are eligible to apply for one of these month-long internships. Young people considering careers in the hospitality industry can pursue an internship in hotel management, working alongside the professionals at The Lanesborough, The Langham Hilton, and other world-class hotels in London. You'll learn about all the major hotel concerns, from the front desk to the kitchen to the guest rooms. And you will have the pleasure of weekend excursions, day trips, and special events in and around one of the world's great cities. Internships generally run from late June to late July and cost about $4,500, plus round-trip airfare. The program fee includes tuition, housing, breakfast and dinner, group outings, a Tube pass, and many other expenses. A completed application form and an essay on why you want to participate must be received by the beginning of May. For a copy of the form and further information about this unique opportunity to intern abroad, contact Intern Exchange International.

Intern Exchange International, Ltd.
130 Harold Road
Woodmere, NY 11598-1435
Tel: 516-374-3939

INTERNATIONAL INN

Internship, Volunteer Opportunity

The International Inn, near Cape Cod, offers many possibilities for high school students interested in the field of hospitality and travel. As a hotel that is open 24 hours a day, 365 days a year, the International Inn requires staff in all departments at virtually all times. This means that you cannot only work in an area of special interest to you—front desk, reservations, housekeeping, food service—but that you can do it during the school year. The hotel evaluates applicants for both internships and volunteer positions on a case-by-case basis. Contact the International Inn to discuss their needs and the position and schedule that is right for you.

> **International Inn**
> 662 Main Street
> Hyannis, MA 02601
> Tel: 508-775-5600

MARYLAND SCHOOL OF TRAVEL

Study/Training

If you've got your heart set on a travel career, you can begin training as a travel agent right now through the Maryland School of Travel, established in 1976. Since you'll probably be attending a different school in the daytime, look into the Maryland School of Travel's night classes. They usually run from 7:00 to 10:00 PM on Mondays from February to May. The curriculum covers the basics of the travel industry and use of the popular computer reservation system SABRE. Upon satisfactory completion of the course, you will receive a certificate of graduation approved by the State Board of Higher Education, and the Maryland School of Travel will provide job placement assistance. It also offers a correspondence course similar to its in-house curriculum. Contact the Maryland School of Travel for more information on the options available to you.

> **Maryland School of Travel**
> Roeder Travel, Ltd.
> 9805 York Road
> Cockeysville, MD 21030
> Tel: 410-667-6090
> Email: school@roedertravel.com

MYRTLE BEACH PAVILION AMUSEMENT PARK

Employment Opportunity

The Myrtle Beach Pavilion Amusement Park is a seaside park featuring some 38 rides and 2 new go-cart tracks. The Pavilion employs a total of about 750 workers, most of whom work from mid-March to mid-October, and welcomes young people interested in experiencing this facet of the tourism industry. Most jobs are in ride operations, food services, and games and arcades, with other positions available in admissions and general services. Rates of pay vary, but they start around $6 an hour for new hires. Accommodations in the Myrtle Beach area can be quite costly, so many employees who are not native to the area make arrangements to share rooms with each other and thus reduce expenses. For more information about job availabilities and to learn more about the benefits of working at the Myrtle Beach Pavilion Amusement Park, contact the Pavilion's General Manager.

Myrtle Beach Pavilion Amusement Park
PO Box 2095
Myrtle Beach, SC 29578-2095
Tel: 803-448-6456

NAF ACADEMY OF TRAVEL AND TOURISM PROGRAM

Study/Training

If your high school is pursuing school-to-work initiatives, you may already have heard of the National Academy Foundation (NAF). A nonprofit foundation, it was established in 1989 to promote partnerships between businesses and public high schools. Under NAF's guidance, these partnerships grow into Academies, or schools within schools that focus on such career fields as finance, public service, and—yes—travel and tourism. Hospitality is also included in NAF's Academies of Travel and Tourism, so if you have the opportunity to participate in such an Academy at your school, give it some serious consideration. Participants in NAF's programs have generally enjoyed great success in college and in their careers because they are well prepared for the world of work. If your high school does not have an Academy, it might be worth your while to give your principal information for the National Academy Foundation. Even if he or she is interested, it will take some time to set up a partnership, but it should be worth the wait.

NAF Academy of Travel and Tourism Program
235 Park Avenue South, Seventh Floor
New York, NY 10003
Tel: 212-420-8400
Web: http://www.naf-education.org

NORTHWESTERN PROFESSIONAL OUTFITTERS

Study/Training

Northwestern Professional Outfitters has put together a comprehensive training course that can help you become a professional guide or outfitter. The emphasis here is on hunting, fishing, camping, and the like. The 4-week, 250-hour training course covers topics you'd need to know as an outdoor guide—such as judging a big game hunt, fixing a gas lantern, federal land use policies, first aid and CPR, and the skinning and care of trophies. An additional 2-week program can be tacked on for students who want to expand their abilities in horse and mule shoeing and backcountry camping. If you're not too worn out at the end of the training course, the school claims to have a 100 percent placement record of graduates who decide to go to work in the profession. Northwestern Professional Outfitters' Web site also covers some information about typical pay rates for starting guides, and cautionary/realistic advice that most guides start at the bottom and work their way up. That means you're the one putting tents up in the rain and gutting rainbow trout for dinner. If this sounds like your dream job, you'll probably want to get in touch with Northwestern Professional Outfitters.

Northwestern Professional Outfitters
1765 Pleasant View Drive
Victor, MT 59875
Tel: 888-642-1010 or 406-642-3262
Web: http://www.huntinfo.com/nwestern.htm
Email: Nwestern@Huntinfo.com

NYU CENTER FOR HOSPITALITY AND TOURISM ADMISSION

Study/Training

New York University (NYU) has a special early enrollment program for high school seniors anxious to begin training for a career in hospitality and travel. The program is very selective, accepting only above-average students with strong recommendations from their principals, guidance counselors, and teachers. You must apply during your junior year and, if accepted, attend college in place of your senior year of high school. Those who successfully complete the program earn both their high school degree (awarded after the first year of college) and a Bachelor of Science in Hotel and Tourism Management. Contact New York University for more information about the early enrollment program and for a course catalog with application guidelines.

■NYU Center for Hospitality and Tourism Admission
11 West 42nd Street, Room 518
New York, NY 10003
Tel: 212-998-4555
Web: http://www.sce.nyu.edu/chtta
Email: sp27@is5.nyu.edu

SEA WORLD OF FLORIDA

Employment Opportunity

Sea World of Florida is, of course, *the* place to work if you are interested in marine life and animal care—but it also offers opportunities for young people interested in travel and hospitality. During the summer and the spring and winter holidays, Sea World has special need of area high school students to fill various positions throughout the park. Seasonal employees fill positions in cash control, education and informational services, food service, horticulture, merchandise, operations, and ticket sales. In addition to gaining experience in the tourism industry and improving your people skills, you earn pay well above the minimum wage and enjoy free passes and other perks. To speak to someone about working at Sea World and to request printed information, contact the Human Resources Department.

■Sea World of Florida
Sea World Staffing Center
7007 Sea Harbor Drive
Orlando, FL 32821
Tel: 407-363-2600

SIX FLAGS OVER GEORGIA

Employment Opportunity

Six Flags Over Georgia, opened in 1967, is part of the Six Flags Theme Parks chain. Young people ages fifteen and over can explore the hospitality and travel industry by working in various aspects of operations. High school students work at numerous positions in admissions, rides, park services, entertainment, retail, and administration. All workers are paid weekly (rates of pay vary with position) and receive such perks as free use of the park on days off, free passes for family and friends, and free parking and uniforms. Six Flags Over Georgia also runs an employees-only cafeteria and a number of special events for its workers. The park is open from March through November and offers flexible hours to its employees. Jobs tend to go fast, so call Human Resources early in the year for application information.

◼ **Six Flags Over Georgia**
PO Box 43187
Atlanta, GA 30378
Tel: 770-739-3410
Web: http://www.sixflags.com

TRAVEL EDUCATION CENTER

Study/Training

High school seniors and older adults looking for a comprehensive travel train-ing program might consider studying at the Travel Education Center. Students there take classes on everything from "Tours and Cruises" and "Hotels and Resorts" to "Destinations" and "Car Rentals." Upon completion of the curricu-lum, which includes experience on computer reservation systems SABRE and APOLLO, students receive a Certificate of Travel Training. The Travel Education Center is accredited and approved by various educational bodies and boasts an excellent record of graduate placement. Its main school is located in Cambridge, Massachusetts. There are branches in Nashua, New Hampshire, and Westchester, Illinois, and satellite extensions are in place across Maine, Massachusetts, and New Hampshire. Day, evening, and Saturday classes are available at all locations except the satellite extensions, which host only evening classes. You can complete the day classes in about two months, the evening and Saturday classes in six. Admission is based on prior academic per-formance and a brief interview. Tuition is around $2,000 and loans and schol-arships are available. Open houses are held frequently and are a great way to learn more about the center, its facilities, and whether it is right for you. Call for the dates of upcoming open houses, to request a brochure, or to arrange a per-sonal visit and informational interview.

◼ **Travel Education Center**
100 Cambridge Park Drive
Cambridge, MA 02140-9104
Tel: 800-945-2220 or 617-547-7750
Email: tec@ultranet.com

VALLEYFAIR FAMILY AMUSEMENT PARK

Employment Opportunity

The Valleyfair Family Amusement Park, located just south of Minneapolis, fea-tures over 75 rides as well as the Pepsi IMAX Theater and live entertainment. Valleyfair has a number of job opportunities available to young people, includ-ing several in admissions, clerical, food service, park service, and rides and games. Pay is above minimum wage, many employees receive end-of-season bonuses, and most workers enjoy such perks as free guest passes and employ-ee-only activities. Valleyfair also has a couple of different programs to provide or arrange for housing for its workers. Contact the Human Resources Department for further information and an application form.

■ **Valleyfair Family Amusement Park**
One Valleyfair Drive
Shakopee, MN 55379
Tel: 800-386-7433 or 612-445-7600
Web: http://www.valleyfair.com

WORLDS OF FUN/OCEANS OF FUN

Employment Opportunity

Worlds of Fun and Oceans of Fun are jointly owned theme parks offering plenty of employment opportunities for young people ages fifteen and over. Employees are referred to as *ambassadors,* and work in many different areas of tourism: admissions, food operations, rides and games, park services, and clerical positions. Wages are competitive (but vary with age and position) and you may also be able to earn a bonus. When you're not working at Worlds of Fun or Oceans of Fun, you could be enjoying the rides at both parks for free or attending one of the many special activities planned for ambassadors. Interviews start in February for these popular jobs, so contact the Human Resources department early for application information.

■ **Worlds of Fun/Oceans of Fun**
4545 Worlds of Fun Avenue
Kansas City, MO 64161
Tel: 816-454-4545

11
Do It Yourself

Katie knew she wanted to work in a hotel. She loved the atmosphere, the energy, and of course, the glamour of hotels. (At least that's the way hotels are portrayed in made-for-TV movies.) At fifteen, Katie didn't have much exposure to different lodging establishments, other than the Holiday Inn for family vacations. "Well, there is time enough for serious career moves," Katie thought. "After all, I'm only in high school."

Samantha knew she wanted to work in a hotel. She, like Katie, loved the atmosphere, the energy, and of course, the glamour of hotels. Samantha, also fifteen years old, didn't have much exposure to different lodging establishments, but was determined to learn as much as possible. "High school is the best time to learn and make good career moves," Samantha thought. "It's never too early to get a head start."

Who do you think is going places? Put your money on Samantha—never before have there been so many possibilities and opportunities available, and in some cases, tailored to high school students interested in entering the hospitality industry. Set yourself apart from the typical Katie. Build your resume—substance not only exists in part-time hotel jobs, but also in setting up your own business, feeding an interest with summer classes, gathering a group of teens with a similar interest in hospitality careers, or earning class credits and pocket money while learning more about the hospitality industry. Education is important, but so are experience and determination. You'll need all three to succeed in this industry.

WHAT CAN YOU DO NOW?

START A CLUB

If you're lucky enough to attend a school with a hospitality and travel club, all you have to do is join up. But if, like most schools, yours does not have such a club, the thing to do is start one. You're probably familiar with a French club or science club, where the goals are to learn more about the subject, to interact with professionals who have experience in the subject, and to have a good time with others who share a common interest. Those are the exact goals of your hospitality and travel club. To learn more, you and your classmates in the club can share books and magazine articles or surf the Internet for information on hospitality and travel careers. To interact with professionals, you can invite a flight attendant to speak to your club or ask a concierge to arrange a tour of his or her hotel. And as you work on these and other projects together, you're bound to have a good time!

Every high school has a different procedure for establishing a club, so check with your principal or guidance counselor to see if there are any formal requirements and to learn how it's been done in the past. In every school, however, the most important elements in a new club are members and a faculty advisor. Ask a teacher to serve as your advisor or sponsor, bearing in mind that if school regulations require him or her to attend club meetings, you'll have to plan your schedule around the teacher's. Be flexible when dealing with faculty, and remember that they're even more pressed for time than you are.

You'll also need at least two or three other students who are interested in careers in hospitality and travel to get your club started. Ask around school to find out who's interested. If there doesn't seem to be much interest at first, you'll need to create some. Tell others about the club between classes, at lunch, during homeroom. Do your homework and share your knowledge of the opportunities the industry has to offer. Write about it in the school newspaper, hang up posters to announce meetings, and make sure that everyone knows about your new club!

GET A JOB

Having a part-time job, no matter how small or tedious, is a good way to set yourself apart from the rest of the pack. You may really want to work the front desk, but if the only opening is for the switchboard, take the job anyway! Prove yourself a hard worker, and you'll be sitting behind the front counter soon enough. Dan, a junior from Palos Heights, Illinois, works part-time at a local business hotel. He wants a future in hotel management, but for now he tallies and stocks the mini-bars. What do pop cans and cashew snack packs have to do with running a hotel? Well . . . looking at the big picture, both jobs require careful planning, record keeping, and judgment. More importantly, working hard at such a routine, entry-level job clearly demonstrates just how committed Dan is to a job in hospitality. Since Dan's supervisors are aware of his hard work and potential, his days of counting candy bars are numbered.

The "Get Involved" section lists a few hotels and travel agencies that offer part-time work for high school students, but don't limit your options to just these places. The classified ads in your city's newspaper should list similar job openings in your area, but you don't have to wait for an opening to be advertised. Target the places where you would like to work. Make a quick phone call to the main number of the hotel or agency to get the name and title of the human resources director. Now sit down and write that person a brief letter. Tell him or her about your interest in a future career in travel and hospitality and why working for their business will help you. Politely indicate that you are interested in any part-time, entry-level positions that may be available now or in the next few months. Add that you will call back in a week to follow up. Tell them that you look forward to speaking with them soon. Before you mail your letter, ask your English teacher to proofread your letter. Include a one-page resume if you have one. After you've mailed your letter, wait a week and make that follow-up call. Introduce yourself, mention your letter, and politely ask if the person has a few minutes to discuss employment opportunities. Even if there is nothing available, if you have made a good impression, you now have a contact in the travel and hospitality business! Ask if it's okay to check back in a few months. Another alternative is to ask your new contact for an information interview to learn more about the industry and its employment opportunities.

You must be prepared to accept the fact that the hotels or travel agencies you contact may have a firm policy about not hiring high school students. Don't let this discourage you from looking elsewhere. The more active you are in looking for a job, the sooner you're likely to find one.

CLEAN UP YOUR ACT

Cleaning chores may be a low priority on many teens' lists of things to do. But if you are one of the few (there are some out there!) who love to clean and are good at it, then you might consider becoming a hotel executive housekeeper. The executive housekeeper holds one of a hotel's highest management positions, overseeing the work of different departments, and taking responsibility for the cleanliness of the entire hotel.

Naturally, the best way to get experience—and make valuable contacts—is to work part-time in the housekeeping department of a hotel. You may not be given actual guest-room assignments; these are usually trusted to trained room attendants. The Sheraton Hotel and Towers in Chicago, Illinois, hires high school students during school breaks to help out with the laundry. Don't belittle this job—the laundry department is responsible for washing everything from bed sheets to staff uniforms. That's about 98,000 pounds of laundry a week! Your local hotel might not have quite *that* much laundry for you to tackle, but they may have work for you just the same.

Another option is to join a cleaning service as a seasonal or part-time worker. Look in the phone book or the newspaper classifieds for listings of cleaning businesses in your area. Many operations, such as McMaid Cleaning Service, are franchised businesses, each responsible for hiring and training their crews. You will be taught good cleaning techniques that also save time and effort. Finding ways to streamline cleaning times is an important duty of an executive housekeeper, and this kind of professional experience would be a real asset.

Of course, ambition and initiative are major assets, too, so you might even consider setting up your own cleaning business. Make fliers describing your services—total house cleaning or special cleaning chores—and your fees. Will you be charging by the hour or by the chore? If you will bring all cleaning supplies and the vacuum cleaner, then charge a little extra to cover your overhead. If you aren't sure about how much to charge, ask around to get an idea of how much a cleaning person charges for cleaning, say a three-bedroom, two-bath townhouse. Distribute the flyers to your family, neighbors, seniors, and friends. It may be a good idea to advertise in your community or school paper, as well as church bulletins. Professionals never miss an appointment and are always on time, so note your cleaning jobs in an appointment book to keep yourself organized. Don't limit yourself to homes—cleaning opportunities can be found in small businesses and offices and churches, as well as yards and cars.

TRAVEL ABROAD

If you want to assist travelers—as a tour guide, travel agent, or concierge—then one of the best ways to gain professional experience is, of course, by traveling. Yes, vacationing with your family certainly does count as travel. Just by flying off to a Holiday Inn a couple of states away, you should be able to observe and maybe even speak to people working in every occupation profiled in this book. But traveling abroad can give you a better, broader experience of the hospitality and travel industry—and you don't have to travel with Mom and Dad to get there.

Is your school's French club going to Paris or the Spanish club to Madrid to brush up on their language skills? If so, will you be with them or will you be sitting at home while they meet flight attendants, hotel desk clerks, and other hospitality and travel workers from around the world? Does the college you plan to attend sponsor a junior year abroad, allowing you to live and study in a foreign country for one or two semesters? Does your church or another local organization sponsor foreign exchanges, where you and a young person from another country swap homes for a month or more? If you answered "yes" to any of these questions—and you probably did—then traveling abroad may be in your not-too-distant future.

GIVE THEM THE GRAND TOUR

Holly Stiel, one of the first female concierges in the United States, started her career selling tickets at a San Francisco tour booth. Before long, tourists were lined up around her booth for reasons other than buying tickets. Tourists approached Holly for directions to city sights and trusted her advice on "must see" attractions in San Francisco. If you constantly play tour guide for out-of-town relatives, or if your friends ask for suggestions on what to do every Saturday night, then you probably have the makings of a *tour guide* or *hotel concierge.*

You might seek out a formal position as a tour guide with your city's tourist office or chamber of commerce. If they don't have such a position, you can volunteer to create one. Research your town's history, bearing in mind the kind of questions people usually ask about buildings, landmarks, and famous people. Plan a tour—anywhere from thirty minutes to two hours, depending on the size of your town—incorporating this history and your knowledge of current happenings. Then arrange to present this tour to officials from the tourist office or chamber of commerce and try to work together to present this tour to the public. Perhaps you could place fliers in the tourist office announcing that you will lead the tours every hour on the hour on Saturday afternoons. This is a lot of work, but one day it could be your career!

If you're looking for something a little less challenging, why not gain experience as a tour guide in a local museum, park, or historical site? The principles of guiding visitors are just the same, and such establishments are usually very welcoming toward young people. You might also be able to act as a tour guide in your own school by showing it off and sharing your inside information with new and visiting students. Speak with your principal about becoming the school's official tour guide; classmates who share your career interests could help you build a club or organization on that premise.

SHADOWING THE PROS

As you already know, the best way to learn if a career is right for you is to experience it, even for a day. Many schools have implemented job-shadowing programs in which students' interests are matched to area businesses. Students from one Illinois high school wanted to learn more about the hotel industry, so they were able to spend a few afternoons "shadowing" actual employees of a nearby hotel. Many teens may want to be in a top position such as a hotel general manager, but may not be aware of the duties and responsibilities associated with the job. In addition to experiencing a typical day alongside a front desk manager, hotel general manager, and reservation clerk, the students are able to ask questions and help out when possible.

As ever, you shouldn't be discouraged if your school lacks a formal job-shadowing program. One option is to work with your principal or guidance counselor to start such a program. It will take a good deal of planning but, when presented with solid facts, dates, and times, both students and businesses are usually willing to participate. Another option is for you to strike out on your own. If you want to be a travel agent, ask your relatives and their friends if they can put you in touch with a professional travel agent. You can then ask to be allowed to shadow that travel agent while he or she is at work, perhaps on a Saturday afternoon. Or you can write a letter to a local travel agency, explaining your career goals and your desire to shadow an agent. Again, persistence and politeness are the key.

CONCLUSION

These are just some ways to explore and train for a career in hospitality and travel. The important factor in each of them is a willingness to do something different, something that hasn't been done before in your school or in your community. It won't always be easy. Some of your requests will be rejected and some of your tasks will be nerve-racking. But your efforts *will* pay off—trying new things and meeting new people are always to your benefit, though not always in obvious ways. It's worth taking a chance because it's your future.

Surf the Web

FIRST

You must use the Internet to do research, to find out, to explore. The Internet is the closest you'll get to what's happening right now around the world. This chapter gets you started with an annotated list of Web sites related to hospitality and travel. Try a few. Follow the links. Maybe even venture as far as asking questions in a chat room. The more you read about and interact with personnel in this field, the better prepared you'll be when you're old enough to participate as a professional.

One caveat: you probably already know that URLs change all the time. If a Web address listed below is out of date, try searching on the site's name or other key-words. Chances are, if it's still out there, you'll find it. If it's not, maybe you'll find something better!

THE SITES

COOL CAREERS

http://www.pbs.org/jobs/careers/jump.html

Sponsored by the Public Broadcasting Service (PBS), this enthusiastic site was developed to get teens thinking about their future careers. And it just so happens to spotlight the career of an American Airlines pilot. Even if this isn't exactly the kind of travel career you have in mind, you'll learn a great deal from a lengthy profile on how he developed his talents to reach his career dream. The pilot's biographical sketch is a first-person narrative exploring his background from childhood to the present day. Subsequent pages go into detail about how he pursued his career and what his job actually entails. One of the best features at this site is that after you've read through the sections, you can actually email the pilot to ask him career questions.

COUNCIL ON HOTEL, RESTAURANT & INSTITUTIONAL EDUCATION
http://chrie.org/

This site has an appealing home page that invites you to explore further. For openers, you probably want to know what the Council on Hotel, Restaurant & Institutional Education (CHRIE) *does*. In a nutshell, it's a nonprofit association instrumental in standardizing and improving the education and training of people in the hospitality and travel industries. Many of the topics you'll find at this site (like accreditation of training programs) are pretty esoteric at this stage of your career. But other sections, like the chatty news articles, impart a sense of how much fun this profession can be. This site also reveals CHRIE's real commitment to its student members. At a recent national conference, three separate events emphasized students' interactions with industry recruiters and other professionals in the field. CHRIE has also created a booklet that spells out the necessary knowledge, skills, and abilities for these jobs: front desk associates, reservations agents, concierges, and bellpersons. If you're interested, there's a number to call to receive a free copy. Finally, what Web site would be complete without a chat room? Click on the button Forums and Chats and you'll be transported to the Hospitality and Tourism Global Forum, a discussion group that tends to be on the academic side of the fence.

CYBERAIR AIRPARK
http://www.cyberair.com/index.html

It's worth your while to download RealAudio and RealVideo when you visit this site, because it aims to give you a sensory aviation experience. The site was put together by pilots and aviation buffs, and it's a refreshing combination of safety-related information and plain old fun stuff. From the home page's graphic of a landing runway, you can click on pages that will let you simulate flight on a helicopter or eavesdrop on air traffic controllers on the Chicago Approach frequency, transmitted from O'Hare Airport. There's a map on-line to help you track the airports that you'll hear mentioned in the transmissions. Back on CyberAir's home page, you can listen to a recording from the Voyager aircraft making its record-breaking flight around the world in 1986 without landing or refueling. Be sure to visit the section devoted to aviation safety, where there are lots of downloadable videos by the Federal Aviation Administration (FAA), plus a section called "I Want to Be a Pilot." Inside this section, you can read the FAA's

"Flying Start" guide, which walks you through how to become a pilot and what it's like to learn to fly.

DEPARTMENT OF HOSPITALITY MANAGEMENT
AT THE UNIVERSITY OF NEW HAMPSHIRE
http://orbit.unh.edu/dhm/index.htm

If you're searching for a university or training program to help you with your career in hospitality, this site is worth a look. While there are probably hundreds of schools shopping their wares on-line, this site from the University of New Hampshire's (UNH) Department of Hospitality Management stands out for its thorough course descriptions, strong internship program, and surprisingly unbiased advice on choosing a school.

The most natural place to start is a section called "Hospitality Education." It's a primer for high school students on how to compare degree programs when choosing a college. Sure, there are plenty of plugs for UNH here, but there's also impartial data like the Hospitality Education Program Rating System, a methodology created by the Council on Hotel, Restaurant and Institutional Education. And there are even links to over twenty other colleges and universities that offer hospitality-related degrees.

To find out what UNH thinks is special about their program, go back to the home page and click on Highlights. Here, you'll read a description of the four-year bachelor's degree that prepares students for management positions in hotels, resorts, restaurants, and other tourism-related businesses. There's even nitty-gritty information about course requirements and placement services. The faculty has also pulled together an impressive index of hundreds of sites on the Web. This may not be the college for you, but you'll consult this site for all kinds of hospitality-related information.

FLIGHT ATTENDANT CORPORATION OF AMERICA
http://www.flightattendantcorp.com/

This straightforward site will tell you what it takes to become a flight attendant. Click on Minimum Requirements if you're wondering whether you're old enough, tall enough, or educated enough. You'll be pleasantly surprised to learn that the airlines no longer have the stringent requirements they did in the past. A page called "Frequently Asked Questions" is the best place to start exploring this site. Here, you'll find out about salaries, flight benefits, and typical training. To see which airlines are currently hiring, look no further than Who's Hiring, a section that also explains how and when to contact various major, regional, and commuter airlines. Once you've lined up an interview, you'll appreciate another section that offers sample interview questions (and the answers that the airlines want to hear).

If you like what you find at this site and want more . . . well, that's the idea. The Flight Attendant Corporation sells a book, written by a former United Airlines flight attendant, that covers all of these topics in much greater detail. Just hand over a credit card number to have it sent to you. The only remaining freebie at this site is the Resource Center, which has links to many airline Web sites, including United, TWA, American, and Conair.

FUNSTUFF INTERNSHIP PROGRAM

http://members.aol.com/funstufinc/index.html

This internship program in Recreation and Leisure Management is hard to ignore. Instead of spending a summer working at the local taco restaurant, you could be learning skills that will come in handy later, like community first aid, emergency water safety, recordkeeping, and travel marketing. And you get to hang out in Myrtle Beach, South Carolina, in the summertime. Seriously, if you want a career in the tourism industry, an internship is invaluable. The positions that were posted on-line fell under the categories of hotel recreation, water park recreation, physical education, aquatics, and crafts. In addition to paying decent wages, some of the positions actually count toward college credits. Unfortunately, there were no detailed job descriptions available. There is, however, an 800 number to call for more information. You can also go directly to the on-line application form if you're gung-ho and ready to apply. For general information about Myrtle Beach, click on the icon at the bottom of the home page.

HOSPITALITY NET

http://www.hospitalitynet.nl/

Welcome to a site that aims to uncover all the nooks and crannies of the hospitality industry for you. The home page is straightforward and introduces you to the site's six major sections. One of these sections—News, Trends and Facts—dishes up breaking headlines in the industry, and provides a database where you can search past articles by keywords. Another section called the Virtual Job Exchange has an excellent selection of internships for students. To get a complete listing, just type "internship" into the search engine and click. Finally, if you don't find what you want elsewhere, check out the Hospitality Index. It's a well-organized resource that can help you locate on-line hospitality discussion groups or explore schools with programs in this field. You can also get the address of virtually any hotel here.

NATIONJOBS NETWORK: HOTEL, RESTAURANT & TRAVEL

http://www.nationjob.com/

This is the home page of the NationJobs Network, an on-line job search service that just happens to have oodles of positions posted for people looking for work in the hospitality and travel industries. If you're impatient with these massive job databases, then go directly to www.nationjob.com/hotel, where you'll find a list that's been whittled down to just jobs in hotels, restaurants, and travel. However, you might want to fine tune your search even more, by searching for a particular job or limiting the search to the part of the country where you live. If nothing catches your eye on your first visit to NationJobs, then take advantage of an excellent free service called P. J. (Personal Job) Scout. Just fill out a form and P. J. will email you descriptions of jobs that just might be what you're looking for.

RESORT, RECREATION & TOURISM MANAGEMENT

http://www.ipcc.com/market/rrtm/page1.html

If you're searching for a really good internship, then pay a visit to this site. It's sponsored by Resort, Recreation & Tourism Management (RRTM), a firm that's contracted by large hotels and resorts to place students in resort, recreation, and tourism jobs year-round. The kinds of internships available include activities coordinator, front desk assistant, hospitality hostess, and so on. These internships aim to provide students with experience and education; interns are required to attend weekly training seminars, complete with guest speakers and homework. Interns are provided with housing and utilities, plus a monthly scholarship of $150 to $300. At some locations, meals might even be thrown into the deal.

Do well in your internship and you'll be encouraged to keep coming back for more. Opportunities to advance through the training program include doing a second internship, becoming a supervisor, then going through management training to work as a manager or director. Job placement after graduation is guaranteed to outstanding interns who have exhibited "enthusiasm, responsibility, and leadership." To get you started, there's an on-line application form. What are you waiting for?

SITES ALIVE!

http://www.oceanchallenge.com/

If travel is a passion for you, then you'll fall in love with this site. It documents the learning adventures of junior high and high school students who are participants in semester-long field trips to far-flung places. Current and recent trips are described in brief, accompanied by a photo and a few quotes by students on the trip. Click on a trip that interests you—perhaps the one to the Australian rain forest—and you'll find even more information. Each week of the trip, students post their journal entries and assigned essays, and they also answer your questions on-line. Students who were visiting South Caicos Island in the Caribbean Sea wrote essays one week examining how tourism impacts the local economy and its effect on the coral reefs there. Even though you may feel envious of these students, they try not to rub it in your face. For each trip, there's a "packet" of suggested activities that you can do to participate from home (admittedly, it's not quite the same as being on a tropical island). Curiously, the one thing that is extremely hard to find at this site is information on how to join up for a semester.

UNITED AIRLINES FLIGHT ATTENDANT CAREER INFORMATION

http://www.ualservices.com/

This is a matter-of-fact site about how to become a flight attendant for one of the nation's largest airlines. Except for a strangely ominous image of a plane approaching a snowcapped mountain on the home page, there aren't a lot of surprises here. But there is excellent information. The topics covered in brief include image, duties, age, language, vision, height and reach, citizenship, and relocation after training. The text goes into some detail about the selection process, which involves two interviews and a physical examination. After being hired, new flight attendants attend a seven-week, tuition-free training program in suburban Chicago. There's a section describing the many benefits of being a flight attendant. Who wouldn't like getting free flights for themselves, their spouses, dependent children, and parents after only six months of employment? But there's bad news, too. You know those uniforms? Expect to shell out about $700 for one if you're chosen to fly United. This site doesn't include an on-line application form, so you'll have to pick up the phone and find out when the next application open house is near you.

Read a Book

FIRST

When it comes to finding out about the travel and hospitality industry, don't overlook a book. (You're reading one now, after all.) What follows is a short, annotated list of books and periodicals related to travel and hospitality. The books range from fiction to personal accounts of what it's like to be a restaurant manager or pilot, to professional volumes on specific topics, such as how to run a bed and breakfast. Don't be afraid to check out the professional journals, either. The technical stuff may be way above your head right now, but if you take the time to become familiar with one or two, you're bound to pick up some of what is important to travel and hospitality personnel, not to mention begin to feel like a part of their world, which is what you're interested in, right?

We've tried to include recent materials as well as old favorites. Always check for the most recent editions, and, if you find an author you like, ask your librarian to help you find more. Keep reading good books!

BOOKS

Alonzo, Roy S. *The Upstart Guide to Owning and Managing a Restaurant.* Chicago: Upstart Publishing Co., 1996. Written by a professor of food service management, this book provides step-by-step strategies and action plans for understanding and managing restaurant staff, ensuring profitability, and creating ambiance.

Brown, Duane. *Flying Without Fear.* Oakland: New Harbinger Publications, 1996. Shows how to confront flight anxiety with step-by-step techniques. Great for pilots and travelers alike.

Carter, Jimmy. *An Outdoor Journal.* Fayetteville: University of Arkansas Press, 1995. The former president's funny and entertaining reflections on dangers in the woods, fly-fishing, learning to hunt, adventures in New Zealand and Kilimanjaro, and more.

Chatwin, Bruce. *What Am I Doing Here?* New York: Penguin, 1989. Collection of profiles, travelogues, and stories from a great traveler, adventurer, and literary craftsman.

Chemlynski, Carol Anne Caprione. *Opportunities in Restaurant Careers.* Lincolnwood: NTC Publishing Group, 1990. Comprehensive book written by a veteran of food service. Provides practical overview of the field, from education requirements to working conditions.

Christy, Joe. *Your Pilot's License.* 5th ed. Blue Ridge Summit: TAB Books, 1994. Quintessential guide for aspiring and novice pilots. Outlines the ins and outs of flight education, from takeoff to landing.

Craig, Patricia, ed. *The Oxford Book of Travel Stories.* Oxford: Oxford University Press, 1996. Brings together superb short fiction, from Charles Dickens and Evelyn Waugh to John Cheever and Diane Johnson, about living and working abroad.

del Giudice, Daniele. *Takeoff: The Pilot's Lore.* Translated by Joseph Farrell. New York: Harcourt Brace, 1996. Meditations on flying that interweave the observations and dreams of a great writer and aeronaut.

Forsyth, Frederick, ed. *Great Flying Stories.* New York: W. W. Norton & Co., 1991. Collection of enchanting stories about flying by H. G. Wells, J. G. Ballard, John Buchan, Sir Arthur Conan Doyle, and others.

Griffin, Jeff. *Becoming an Airline Pilot.* Blue Ridge Summit: TAB Books, 1990. Standard text. Outlines realistic 10-Step Action Plan for launching a lucrative and rewarding career as an airline pilot. Includes list of colleges and universities with aviation programs.

Gurvis, Sandra. *The Off-the-Beaten Path Job Book: You Can Make a Living and Have a Life!* New York: Carol Communications, 1995. Sections on "The Great Outdoors" and "Travel Mavens" are useful references for finding jobs in adventure and travel.

Hawkes, John K. *Career Opportunities in Travel and Tourism.* New York: Facts on File, 1995. Covers travel agency and coordination, hotel and hotel restaurant management, hotel administration, casino operations, theme parks, cruises, and car rentals.

Hewson, Robert, ed. *The Vital Guide to Commercial Aircraft and Airliners.* Shrewsbury: Airlife Publishing, 1994. Colorful and informative guide to airplanes and major airlines.

Hiam, Alex and Susan Angle. *Adventure Careers: Your Guide to Exciting Jobs, Uncommon Occupations and Extraordinary Experiences.* 2d ed. Hawthorne: Career Press, 1995. Covers wilderness experiences, spiritual work abroad, and many types of overseas adventures.

Krakauer, Jon. *Into Thin Air.* New York: Villard Books, 1997. A tremendously exciting first-person account of the perils faced by climbers and their guides on Mount Everest.

Krannich, Ronald L. and Caryl Rae Krannich. *Jobs for People Who Love to Travel.* Manhassas Park: Impact Publications, 1995. Great resource for the career-seeker who won't "settle down." Covers anything from teaching English abroad to transportation work.

Maltzman, Jeffrey. *Jobs in Paradise.* Rev. ed. New York: HarperCollins Publishers, 1993. Lists over two hundred thousand jobs in the United States, Canada, the South Pacific, and the Caribbean. Details the drawbacks and perks of exotic working life.

Mayle, Peter. *Hotel Pastis: A Novel of Provence.* New York: Vintage, 1993. A novel of romance about a burnt-out advertising executive who leaves England to transform an abandoned police station into an elegant hotel. Funny and entertaining.

Michael, Angie. *Best Impressions in Hospitality: Your Professional Image for Excellence.* Manhassas Park: Impact Publications, 1995. Covers the entire spectrum of making a good impression in an increasingly global society and multicultural world.

Milne, Robert Scott. *Opportunities in Travel Careers.* Lincolnwood: NTC Publishing Group, 1996. Complete information on many careers in land, air, and sea travel.

Morris, Mary, ed., in collaboration with Larry Connor. *Maiden Voyages: Writings of Women Travelers.* New York: Vintage, 1993. From Edith Wharton on Marrakech to Joan Didion on Bogota, this stunning collection is a must-read for anyone looking to live abroad.

Murphy, Martha Watson. *How to Start and Operate Your Own Bed-and-Breakfast: Down-to-Earth Advice from an Award-Winning B & B Owner.* New York: Henry Holt & Co., 1994. In this interesting guide to starting up a B & B, there is much to be learned about hotel hospitality and maintenance.

Paradis, Adrian A. *Opportunities in Airline Careers.* Lincolnwood: NTC Publishing Group, 1997. Contains everything from updated salary information to the latest air traffic concerns.

Rutherford, Denny G., ed. *Hotel Management and Operations.* 2d ed. New York: Van Nostrand Reinhold, 1995. Comprehensive overview of the hospitality industry, covering housekeeping, front desk management and administration, telecommunications, food service, etc.

Shenk, Ellen. *Outdoor Careers: Exploring Occupations in Outdoor Fields.* Harrisburg: Stackpole Books, 1992. Contains useful sections on careers in camping, sky diving, outfitting, horseback riding, diving, and ski patrolling.

Simer, Peter, and John Sullivan. *The National Outdoor Leadership School's Wilderness Guide.* New York: Simon & Schuster, 1983. Classic guide to wilderness camping and hiking techniques, with an eye to coping and conquering risks. Ideal for both guides and amateurs.

Sims-Bell, Barbara. *Career Opportunities in the Food and Beverage Industry.* New York: Facts on File, 1994. Extremely useful guide that includes a thorough section on resorts, country clubs, and hotels.

Steinstra, Tom. *Sunshine Jobs: Career Opportunities Working Outdoors.* Boulder: Live Oak Publications, 1997. Excellent guide to various careers, from bush pilot to hunting guide to lodge operator, written by *The San Francisco Examiner*'s well-known outdoors writer. Includes pay scales, training and education requirements, and first-person interviews.

Stevens, Lawrence. *Your Career in Travel, Tourism, and Hospitality.* 6th ed. Albany: Delmar Publishers Inc., 1988. Oldie but goodie, covering airlines, travel agencies, tour operations, hotels and motels, food service, etc.

Young-Bruehl, Elisabeth. *Global Cultures: A Transnational Short Fiction Reader.* Hanover: The University Press of New England, 1994. Stories from India, Cuba, South Africa, Uruguay, and many other places that show how cultures around the world converge and diverge.

PERIODICALS

Cornell Hotel and Restaurant Administration. Published quarterly by Cornell University, Ithaca, NY 14850. Leads the field of industry magazines for hotel and restaurant management.

Escape. Published monthly by Escape, 2525 Beverly, Santa Monica, CA 90405. Important magazine celebrating the spirit of the road and travel—the wonders of "participating in the world." Stresses the importance of ecologically responsible tourism.

Executive Housekeeping Today. Published monthly by the National Executive Housekeepers Association, Inc., 1001 Eastwind Drive, Suite 301, Westerville, OH 43081-3361. Filled with first-person accounts and anecdotes about the lives and survival strategies of professional housekeepers.

Flight Journal. Published bimonthly by Air Age Inc., 100 East Ridge, Ridgefield, CT 06877-4606. Explores the ins and outs of various forms of aviation, from commercial to recreational.

Flying. Published monthly by Hachette Filipacchi Magazines, Inc., 1633 Broadway, New York, NY 10019. World's most widely read aviation magazine. Very informative guide to anything from getting certified to the virtues of various flying careers.

Hosteur. Published biannually by the Council on Hotel, Restaurant and Institutional Education (CHRIE), 1200 17th Street, NW, Washington, DC 20036-3097. Only international career and self-development magazine for future hospitality and tourism professionals. Used as a classroom and training resource by many educators.

Lodging. Published monthly by the American Hotel and Motel Association, 1201 New York Avenue, NW, Washington, DC 20005-3931. Covers lodging, hospitality, travel, and tourism from a professional perspective.

Outdoor World. Published bimonthly by Magnolia Media Group, 1227 West Magnolia Avenue., Fort Worth, TX 76104. Mostly through profiles of professional outdoorspeople, takes us on a tour through the various vocations and avocations offered by the great outdoors, especially hunting, fishing, climbing, and camping.

Outpost. Published quarterly by Outpost Productions, 490 Adelaide Street West, #303, Toronto, Canada M5V 1T2. Collects excellent perspectives on food, hotels, and travel, and on film, books, and music related to traveling. Covers four corners of the globe in pursuit of "the personal and experiential" dimension of travel.

Outside. Published monthly by Outside, 400 Market Street, Santa Fe, NM 87501. Essential magazine for adventurers and those in the adventure field; explores tourism through profiles of outposts and expeditions, illuminating the dangers faced by adventure travelers and their guides.

Plane & Pilot. Published monthly by Werner Publishing, 12121 Wilshire Boulevard, #1220, Los Angeles, CA 90025. Addresses topics of interest to piston-engine pilots and others interested in private aviation and aircraft. Of great technical value in shedding light on aviation protocol and machinery.

Resort, Spa, and Hotel Management Online. Web site created by Cygnet Risk Management Services, Inc. (http://www.crminsurance.com). Contains useful information on resorts and spas, legal bulletins, and the latest news in hospitality.

Travel & Holiday. Published monthly by Hachette Filipacchi Magazines, Inc., 1633 Broadway, New York, NY 10019. Directed at travelers and at people in the travel industry. Filled with articles about what makes the best places to visit so special.

Travel Weekly. Published by the Reed Travel Group, 500 Plaza Drive, Secaucus, NJ 07094. Comprehensive, impartial information, essential news and knowledge, put together by the world's largest supplier of travel information. Designed for agents and travelers alike.

Ask for Money

By the time most students get around to thinking about applying for scholarships, they have already extolled their personal and academic virtues to such lengths in essays and interviews for college applications that even their own grandmothers wouldn't recognize them. The thought of filling out yet another application form fills students with dread. And why bother? Won't the same five or six kids who have been fighting over grade point averages since the fifth grade walk away with all the really *good* scholarships?

The truth is, most of the scholarships available to high school and college students are being offered because an organization wants to promote interest in a particular field, encourage more students to become qualified to enter it, and finally, to help those students afford an education. Certainly, having a good grade point average is a valuable asset, and many organizations who grant scholarships request that only applicants with a minimum grade point average apply. More often than not, however, grade point averages aren't even mentioned; the focus is on the area of interest and what a student has done to distinguish himself or herself in that area. In fact, frequently the *only* requirement is that the scholarship applicant must be studying in a particular area.

GUIDELINES

When applying for scholarships there are a few simple guidelines that can help ease the process considerably.

Plan Ahead

The absolute worst thing you can do is wait until the last minute. For one thing, obtaining recommendations or other supporting data in time to meet an application deadline is incredibly difficult. For another, no one does their best thinking or writing under the gun. So get off to a good start by reviewing scholarship applications as early as possible—months, even a year, in advance. If the current scholarship information isn't available, ask for a copy of last year's version. Once you have the scholarship information or application in hand, give it a thorough read. Try to determine how your experience or situation best fits into the scholarship, or even if it fits at all.

If possible, research the award or scholarship, including past recipients and, where applicable, the person in whose name the scholarship is offered. Often, scholarships are established to memorialize an individual who majored in religious studies or loved history, et cetera, but in other cases, the scholarship is to memorialize the *work* of an individual. In those cases, try and get a feel for the spirit of the person's work. If you have any similar interests or experiences, don't hesitate to mention these.

Talk to others who received the scholarship, or to students currently studying in the same area or field of interest in which the scholarship is offered, and try to gain insight into possible applications or work related to that field. When you're working on the essay asking why you want this scholarship, you'll have real answers: "I would benefit from receiving this scholarship because studying engineering will help me to design inexpensive but attractive and structurally sound urban housing."

Take your time writing the essays. Make certain you are answering the question or questions on the application and not merely restating facts about yourself. Don't be afraid to get creative; try to imagine what you would think of if you had to sift through hundreds of applications. What would you want to know about the candidate? What would convince you that someone was deserving of the scholarship? Work through several drafts and have someone whose advice you respect—a parent, teacher, or guidance counselor—review the essay for grammar and content.

Finally, if you know in advance which scholarships you want to apply for, there might still be time to stack the deck in your favor by getting an internship, volunteering, or working part-time. Bottom line: the more you know about a scholarship and the sooner you learn it, the better.

Follow Directions

Think of it this way—many of the organizations who offer scholarships devote 99.9 percent of their time to something other than the scholarship for which you are applying. Don't make a nuisance of yourself by pestering them for information. Follow the directions on an application. If the scholarship information specifies that you write for an application form or for further information, write for it—don't call.

Pay close attention to whether you're applying for an award, a scholarship, a prize, financial aid, et cetera. Often these words are used interchangeably, but just as often they have different meanings. An award is usually given for something you have done: built a park or helped distribute meals to the elderly; or something you have created: a design, an essay, a short film, a screenplay, an invention. On the other hand, a scholarship is frequently a renewable sum of money that is given to a person to help defray the costs of college. Scholarships are given to candidates who meet the necessary criteria based on essays, eligibility, grades, or a combination of the three.

Supply all the necessary documents, information, fees, and other items and make the deadlines. You won't win any scholarships by forgetting to include a recommendation from your guidance counselor or failing to postmark the application by the deadline. Bottom line: get it right the first time, on time.

Apply Early

Once you have the application in hand, don't dawdle. If you've requested it far enough in advance, there shouldn't be any reason for you not to turn it in well in advance of the deadline. You never know, if it comes down to two candidates, your timeliness just might be the deciding factor. Bottom line: don't wait, don't hesitate.

Be Yourself

Don't make promises you can't keep. There are plenty of hefty scholarships available, but if they require you to study something that you don't enjoy, you'll be miserable in college. And the side effects from switching majors after you've accepted a scholarship could be even worse. Bottom line: be yourself.

Don't Limit Yourself

There are many sources for scholarships, beginning with your guidance counselor and ending with the Internet. All of the search engines have education categories. Start there and search by keywords, such as "financial aid," "scholarship," "award." Don't be limited to the scholarships listed in these pages.

If you know of an organization related to or involved with the field of your choice, write a letter asking if they offer scholarships. If they don't offer scholarships, don't let that stop you. Write them another letter, or better yet, schedule a meeting with the president or someone in the public relations office and ask them if they would be willing to sponsor a scholarship for you. Of course, you'll need to prepare yourself well for such a meeting because you're selling a priceless commodity—yourself. Don't be shy, be confident. Tell them all about yourself, what you want to study and why, and let them know what you would be willing to do in exchange—volunteer at their favorite charity, write up reports on your progress in school, or work part-time on school breaks, full-time during the summer. Explain why you're a wise investment. Bottom line: the sky's the limit.

THE LIST

A. L. Simmons Scholarships
American Society of Travel Agents
1101 King Street
Alexandria, VA 22314
Tel: 703-739-2782

Applicant must submit upper-level paper or thesis (fifteen to fifty pages) on a travel and tourism topic which has been or will be submitted to a professor. Reapplication is required for renewal. Awarded every year to two recipients, each scholarship is worth $2,000.

Air Travel Card Scholarship
American Society of Travel Agents
1101 King Street
Alexandria, VA 22314
Tel: 703-739-2782

Must be currently studying or planning to study travel management or business management with a minor in tourism or hospitality. The $3,000 award is given to one recipient.

▓ Alaska Airlines Scholarships
American Society of Travel Agents
1101 King Street
Alexandria, VA 22314
Tel: 703-739-2782

Funds are available to undergraduate students who are enrolled in an accredited two- or four-year college or university or a Certified Travel Counselor program. Applicants must be U.S. or Canadian citizens, have a minimum GPA of 2.5, and plan a career in travel or tourism. The $1,000 grant is awarded to three recipients.

▓ American Culinary Federation
10 San Bartolla Road
St. Augustine, FL 32086-3466
Tel: 904-824-4468

The American Culinary Federation makes an annual award, of a variable amount, to an ACF member enrolled in a postsecondary culinary arts program.

▓ American Express and HSMAI Scholarships
Hospitality Sales and Marketing Association International
1300 L Street, NW, Suite 800
Washington, DC 20005
Tel: 202-789-0089

This program is open to full-time students who are currently enrolled in a hospitality-related curriculum. They must have completed at least two years of college, supply two recommendations, and complete three personal essays. Selection is based on work experience, academic studies, extracurricular involvement, presentation of application, response to essay questions, recommendations, and financial status. There are stipends of $3,000 (for the first-place winner) and $1,000 (for the two runners-up).

▓ American Express Travel Scholarships
American Society of Travel Agents
1101 King Street
Alexandria, VA 22314
Tel: 703-739-2782

Funds are available to undergraduate students who are enrolled in an accredited two- or four-year college or university. Applicants must be U.S. or Canadian citizens, have a minimum GPA of 2.5, and plan a career in travel or tourism. A $2,000 grant is awarded to two recipients.

American Hotel Foundation Scholarship
American Hotel Foundation
121 New York Avenue, NW, Suite 600
Washington, DC 20005-3931
Tel: 202-289-3100

This renewable scholarship is available to sophomores, juniors, and seniors. Applicants must be enrolled full-time at an AHF approved two- or four-year college or university. Awarded every year, the amount varies between $500 and $1,000.

Avid Hallissey Memorial Scholarship
American Society of Travel Agents
1101 King Street
Alexandria, VA 22314
Tel: 703-739-2782

Funds are available to undergraduate students who are enrolled in an accredited two- or four-year college or university. Applicants must be U.S. or Canadian citizens, have a minimum GPA of 2.5, and plan a career in travel or tourism. The $1,500 scholarship is awarded to one recipient.

Avis Rent-A-Car Scholarship
American Society of Travel Agents
1101 King Street
Alexandria, VA 22314
Tel: 703-739-2782

Funds are available to undergraduate students who are enrolled in an accredited two- or four-year college or university. Applicants must be U.S. or Canadian citizens, have a minimum GPA of 2.5, and plan a career in travel or tourism. The $1,000 grant is awarded to one recipient.

Boeing Student Research Award
Travel and Tourism Research Association
546 East Main Street
Lexington, KY 40508

Undergraduate and graduate students enrolled in university degree programs are eligible for this award. They must have recently written or be planning to write a research paper on travel or tourism, or a marketing paper concerning travel. The research may deal with primary or secondary data or with a theory. Selection is based on quality of research, creativity of approach, relationship to travel or tourism, usefulness and applicability, and quality of presentation. The $1,000 award is given to one recipient.

Club Managers Association of America
1733 King Street
Alexandria, VA 22314
Tel: 703-739-9500

Grants from the association range from $1,000 to $2,000, and are awarded to sophomores, juniors, or seniors specializing in club management at an accredited college or university.

Dr. Tom Anderson Memorial Scholarship
National Tour Foundation
546 East Main Street
Lexington, KY 40508
Tel: 800-682-8886, ext. 4293

Applicants must be enrolled full-time at a two- or four-year college or university in North America, be entering their junior or senior year of study, have earned at least a 3.0 GPA, be working on a degree in a travel- or tourism-related field, and submit the following: a scholarship application, two letters of recommendation, a resume noting all tourism-related activities, a college transcript, and an essay. The stipend is $2,000. In addition to the scholarship, the winner is given the opportunity to attend the foundation's national convention (the trip is valued at more than $2,000). Plus, the winner receives a one-year subscription to *Courier* magazine, the *Tuesday* newsletter, and the *NTF Headlines* newsletter.

Eric & Bette Friedheim Scholarship
National Tour Foundation
546 East Main Street
Lexington, KY 40508
Tel: 800-682-8886, ext. 4293

Applicants must be enrolled full-time at a four-year college or university in North America, be entering their junior or senior year of study, have earned at least a 3.0 GPA, be working on a degree in a travel- or tourism-related field, and submit the following: a scholarship application, two letters of recommendation, a resume noting all tourism-related activities, a college transcript, and an essay. The stipend is $500. In addition to the scholarship, the winner is given the opportunity to attend the foundation's national convention (the trip is valued at more than $2,000). Plus, the winner receives a one-year subscription to *Courier* magazine, the *Tuesday* newsletter, and the *NTF Headlines* newsletter.

George Reinke Scholarship
American Society of Travel Agents
1101 King Street
Alexandria, VA 22314
Tel: 703-739-2782

Applicants must demonstrate financial need and submit a five hundred-word essay. Reapplication is required for renewal. A $1,000 award is given to three recipients every year.

H. Neil Mecaskey Scholarship
National Tourism Foundation
546 East Main Street
Lexington, KY 40508
Tel: 800-682-8886, ext. 4251

Applicants must be full-time students at a two-year or four-year college or university in North America, be entering their junior or senior year of study, be a strong academic performer, have at least a 3.0 GPA on a 4.0 scale, and have a degree emphasis in a travel- or tourism-related field. The stipend is $500. In addition to the scholarship, the winner is given the opportunity to attend the foundation's national convention (the trip is valued at more than $2,000). Plus, the winner receives a one-year subscription to *Courier* magazine, the *Tuesday* newsletter, and the *NTF Headlines* newsletter.

Healy Scholarship
American Society of Travel Agents
1101 King Street
Alexandria, VA 22314
Tel: 703-739-2782

Funds are available to undergraduate students who are enrolled in an accredited two- or four-year college or university. Applicants must be U.S. or Canadian citizens, have a minimum GPA of 2.5, and plan a career in travel or tourism. The $1,200 grant is awarded to one recipient.

Holland-America Line Westours Scholarship
American Society of Travel Agents
1101 King Street
Alexandria, VA 22314
Tel: 703-739-2782

Applicants must submit a five hundred-word essay on the future of the cruise industry. A $1,200 scholarship is awarded every year to four recipients. Reapplication is required for renewal.

International Association Of Hospitality Accountants Scholarships
PO Box 203008
Austin, TX 78720-3008
Tel: 512-346-5680

Three scholarships are awarded each year to students majoring in either accounting or hospitality management at an accredited college or university. Applications must come through an IAHA local chapter president. The $1,500 award is given to one recipient.

Joseph R. Stone Scholarships
American Society of Travel Agents
1101 King Street
Alexandria, VA 22314
Tel: 703-739-2782

Applicants must be the child of a travel industry employee, have a minimum 3.0 GPA and submit a five hundred-word essay. The $2,400 award is given to two recipients each year. Reapplication is required for renewal.

Louise Dessureault Memorial Scholarship
National Tourism Foundation
546 East Main Street
Lexington, KY 40508
Tel: 800-682-8886, ext. 4251

Applicants must be full-time students at a two- or four-year college or university in North America, be entering their junior or senior year, be strong academic performers with at least a 3.0 GPA on a 4.0 scale, and have a degree emphasis in a travel- or tourism-related field. The stipend is $500. In addition to the scholarship, the winner is given the opportunity to attend the foundation's national convention (the trip is valued at more than $2,000). Plus, the winner receives a one-year subscription to *Courier* magazine, the *Tuesday* newsletter, and the *NTF Headlines* newsletter.

National Tour Foundation Scholarship
546 East Main Street
Lexington, KY 40508
Tel: 800-682-8886, ext. 4293

Available for students enrolled full-time in a tourism-related college with at least a 3.0 GPA.

Northern California/Richard Epping Scholarship
American Society of Travel Agents
1101 King Street
Alexandria, VA 22314
Tel: 703-739-2782

Funds are available to undergraduate students enrolled in an accredited two-
or four-year college or university. Applicants must be U.S. or Canadian citizens
located within the boundaries of the Northern California ASTA Chapter, have a
minimum GPA of 2.5, and be planning a career in travel or tourism. The $1,000
grant is awarded to one recipient.

Perkins Family Restaurant Scholarship
National FFA Center
5632 Mt. Vernon Memorial Highway
PO Box 15160
Alexandria, VA 22309-0160
Tel: 703-360-3600

FFA members who are planning to pursue a college degree in
hotel/motel/institutional management or food science are eligible. They must
be either high school seniors or high school graduates preparing to enroll in
their first year of education beyond high school. Applicants must be from one
of the following thirteen states: Florida, Illinois, Iowa, Kansas, Michigan,
Minnesota, Missouri, Nebraska, North Carolina, North Dakota, Pennsylvania,
Tennessee, and Wisconsin. The stipend is $1,500 per year, paid directly to the
recipient.

Princess Cruises and Princess Tours Scholarships
American Society of Travel Agents
1101 King Street
Alexandria, VA 22314
Tel: 703-739-2782

Applicants must submit a three hundred-word essay on two features that
cruise ships will need to offer passengers in the next ten years. The scholarships are awarded every year to two recipients; each award is worth $1,200.
Reapplication is required for renewal.

Southern California Chapter/Pleasant Hawaiian Holidays Scholarships
American Society of Travel Agents
1101 King Street
Alexandria, VA 22314
Tel: 703-739-2782

Applicants must be U.S. citizens, have a minimum 3.0 GPA, and have at least one parent employed in the travel industry (car rental, airline, travel agency, hotel) in the southern California area. A 1,000-word essay must be submitted with the application. The scholarships are awarded every year to two recipients; each award is worth $1,500.

Student Travel Research Awards
Travel and Tourism Research Association
10200 West 44th Avenue, #304
Wheat Ridge, CO 80033
Tel: 303-940-6557

The Student Travel Research Award ($500) is open to graduate or undergraduate students. Winners also receive an all-expenses-paid trip to TTRA's annual conference.

Tony Orlando Yellow Ribbon Scholarship
National Tour Foundation
546 East Main Street
Lexington, KY 40508
Tel: 800-682-8886, ext. 4293

Applicants must have a physical or sensory disability verified by an accredited physician, be entering college with a 3.0 high school graduate average or have earned at least a 2.5 GPA in a North American college, and be working on a degree in a travel- or tourism-related field. Applicants must submit the following: a scholarship application, two letters of recommendation, a resume noting all tourism-related activities, a college transcript, and an essay. The stipend is $500. In addition to the scholarship, the annual winner is given the opportunity to attend the foundation's national convention (the trip is valued at more than $2,000) plus a one-year subscription to *Courier* magazine, the *Tuesday* newsletter, and the *NTF Headlines* newsletter.

Transportation Clubs International Memorial Scholarships
1275 Kamus Drive, Suite 101
Fox Island, WA 98333
Tel: 206-549-2251

Applicants must be TCI members or dependents of a member. Selection is based upon scholastic ability, potential, professional interest, character, and financial need. A $1,000 award is given to thirty recipients.

▓ Treadway Inns, Hotels, and Resorts Scholarship
National Tour Foundation
546 East Main Street
Lexington, KY 40508
Tel: 800-682-8886, ext. 4293

Applicants must be enrolled full-time at a four-year college or university in North America, be entering their junior or senior year of study, have earned at least a 3.0 GPA, and be working on a degree in a travel- or tourism-related field. Applicants must submit the following: a scholarship application, two letters of recommendation, a resume noting all tourism-related activities, a college transcript, and an essay. The stipend is $500. In addition to the scholarship, the winner is given the opportunity to attend the foundation's national convention (the trip is valued at more than $2,000) and a one-year subscription to *Courier* magazine, the *Tuesday* newsletter, and the *NTF Headlines* newsletter.

Look to the Pros

The following professional organizations offer a variety of materials, from career brochures to lists of accredited schools to salary surveys. Many of them also publish journals and newsletters that you should become familiar with. Many also have annual conferences that you might be able to attend. (While you may not be able to attend a conference as a participant, it may be possible to "cover" one for your school or even your local paper, especially if your school has a related club.)

When contacting professional organizations, keep in mind that they all exist primarily to serve their members, be it through continuing education, professional licensure, political lobbying, or just "keeping up with the profession." While many are strongly interested in promoting their profession and passing information about it to the general public, these busy professional organizations are not there solely to provide you with information. Whether you call or write, be courteous, brief, and to the point. Know what you need and ask for it. If the organization has a Web site, check it out first: what you're looking for may be available there for downloading, or you may find a list of prices or instructions, such as sending a self-addressed, stamped envelope with your request. Finally, be aware that organizations, like people, move. To save time when writing, first confirm the address, preferably with a quick phone call to the organization itself, "Hello, I'm calling to confirm your address. . . ."

THE SOURCES

The Adventure Travel Society
6551 South Revere Parkway, Suite 160
Englewood, CO 80111
Tel: 303-649-9016
Email: ats@adventuretravel.com
Web: http://www.adventuretravel.com/ats

Contact ATS for information on careers in adventure travel, including internships.

Air Line Employees Association
6520 South Cicero
Bedford Park, IL 60638
Tel: 708-563-9999

Contact ALEA for a brochure describing airline jobs.

Air Line Pilots Association International
535 Herndon Parkway
PO Box 1169
Herndon, VA 20172-1169
Tel: 703-481-4440

ALPAI offers *Airline Pilot Career Information*, 20 pages, which is designed for students interested in a career in aviation. It provides an introduction to aviation, describes the three pilot positions and how to prepare for an airline pilot career, discusses licensing requirements, and provides sources of additional information. ALPAI also offers a *Directory of Collegiate Aviation Programs and Options* and a *Flight School Directory*.

Air Transport Association of America
1301 Pennsylvania Avenue, NW, Suite 1100
Washington, DC 20004-1707
Tel: 202-626-4000
Web: http://www.air-transport.org

ATAA offers *The People of the Airlines*, 8 pages, which details the necessary skills, education, and types of careers in the field and contains a list of ATA member airlines. *Where to Find an Aviation Degree*, 4 pages, contains contact information on schools offering aviation degrees, as well as a list of aviation scholarships. The ATAA Web site has a large number of useful airline- and air travel-related links.

■**American Hotel Foundation (AHF)**
Washington, DC 20005-3931
Tel: 202-289-3180
Web: http://www.ahma.com

Contact the AHF for general information on scholarships.

■**American Hotel & Motel Association**
1407 South Harrison Road
PO Box 1240
East Lansing, MI 48826-1240
Tel: 800-344-3320 or 517-353-5500
Web: http://www.ahma.com

AH&MA offers *Lodging and Food Service Careers: A World of Opportunities*, 14 pages, which discusses career opportunities in the field and lists sources of additional information.

■**American Society of Travel Agents**
1101 King Street, Suite 200
Alexandria, VA 22314
Tel: 703-739-2782
Web: http://www.astanet.com/

ASTA offers *ASTA Travel School Members*, 17 pages, *Choosing a Travel School*, 1 page, and *Off to the Right Start with ASTA*, 12 pages, which describes the field, training, agencies, etc.

■**Association for International Practical Training**
10400 Little Patuxent Parkway, Suite 250
Columbia, MD 21044-3510
Tel: 410-997-2200
Web: http://www.aipt.org

AIPT offers *Training for a Global Economy*, 6 pages, which describes the international training opportunities available through three key programs: the Student Exchanges Program for university students, providing on-the-job work experience overseas in a number of technical fields; Career Development Exchanges for trainees with a background in their fields; and Hospitality/Tourism Exchanges, allowing students and graduates of the field to train overseas in the hotel, food service, or travel/tourism fields.

■**Association of Flight Attendants**
1625 Massachusetts Avenue, NW
Washington, DC 20036
Tel: 202-328-5400

AFA offers *Selected United States Airlines,* 4 pages, which lists U.S. airlines (including contact information) that may be accepting flight attendant applications.

■ **Coopers & Lybrand**
1800 M Street, NW
Washington, DC 20036
202-822-4000

C & L offers *United States Nationals Working Abroad: Tax and Other Matters,* $2, 48 pages, which answers questions regarding the income tax implications of working abroad.

■ **Council on Hotel, Restaurant and Institutional Education**
1200 17th Street, NW
Washington, DC 20036-3097
Tel: 202-331-5990
Web: http://chrie.org/

CHRIE offers *United States and International Directory of Schools,* listing schools with programs in hotel and restaurant management, food service management, and the culinary arts.

■ **Council on International Educational Exchange**
205 East 42nd Street
New York, NY 10017-5706
Tel: 212-822-2600
Web: http://www.ciee.org

CIEE offers *Student Travels Magazine,* 48 pages, which includes information on studying, working, and traveling abroad for students. *Students Work Abroad,* 27 pages, describes working abroad opportunities for college students.

■ **The Ecotourism Society**
PO Box 755
North Bennington, VT 05257
Tel: 802-447-2121
Email: ecomail@ecotourism.org
Web: http://www.ecotourism.org

Contact TES for information on the ecotourism industry, as well as information on education and training.

■ **Educational Foundation of the National Restaurant Association**
250 South Wacker Drive, Suite 1400
Chicago, IL 60606-5834
Tel: 800-765-2122 or 312-715-1010
Web: http://www.restaurant.org/educate/educate.htm

EFNRA offers *Choose Foodservice: A Guide to Careers with a Future,* 12 pages, which discusses career options in the foodservice industry, salaries and wage rates, education and training, and financial aid. *Choose Foodservice: A Guide to Two-Year and Four-Year Colleges and Universities with Foodservice/Hospitality Programs,* 46 pages, contains a list of schools with foodservice and hospitality programs.

■ **Federal Aviation Administration**
Superintendent of Documents
Retail Distribution Division
Consigned Branch
8610 Cherry Lane
Laurel, MD 20707
Web: http://www.faa.gov

The following brochures from the FAA Aviation Career Series may be obtained by writing to the FAA. *Pilots and Flight Engineers, Flight Attendants, Airline Non-Flying Careers, Aircraft Manufacturing, Aviation Maintenance and Avionics, Airport Careers,* and *Government Careers.* Write to the Aviation Education Offices, Aviation Education Resource Center, for the following: *Women in Aviation and Space,* $2.50, 21 pages, which profiles 46 women involved in various aviation and space careers, including general flight, federal government, space, education/training, engineering, airport management, aircraft maintenance/air traffic control, business/manufacturing, and the arts in aviation.

■ **Flight Training Magazine**
201 Main Street
Parkville, MO 64152-3733
Tel: 816-741-5151

FTM offers *Choosing a Flight School: A Checklist for Finding Quality Training,* 12 pages, which contains general guidance information. It is intended as an aid for anyone interested in learning to fly and for selecting the training organization that will meet specific needs. *Why College? Because Pilots Do More Than Just Fly,* 7 pages, describes the aviation professional and the necessary education. *Learn to Fly ... Stop Dreaming and Start Flying,* 30 pages, is an excerpt from *Flight Training Magazine.* It includes a flight school directory. *How to Select an Aviation College,* 4 pages, is a checklist for choosing an aviation college that meets specific needs. *Internships and Co-Ops,* 16 pages, is an excerpt from *Flight Training Magazine* that contains information on internships and co-ops in aviation and includes a college directory. *Collegiate Aviation: Programs and Options,* 8 pages, is an excerpt from *Flight Training Magazine* that discusses associate's and bachelor's degree programs, tuition, and finding work. *Flight Training Magazine,* $3.95/copy, is available at local newsstands.

▓ Future Aviation Professionals of America
4959 Massachusetts Boulevard
Atlanta, GA 30337
1-800-JET-JOBS

The Future Aviation Professionals of America can help members by supplying job reports, an employment guide, a directory of employers, and a salary survey. It also provides toll-free interview briefings and a resume service.

▓ Hospitality Sales & Marketing Association International
1300 L Street, NW, Suite 10120
Washington, DC 20005
Tel: 202-789-0089
Web: http://www.hsmai.org/

Check out HSMAI's publications to get an idea of what today's hospitality sales & marketing professional is interested in.

▓ Hosteling International—American Youth Hostels
733 15th Street, NW, Suite 840
Washington, DC 20005
Tel: 202-783-6161

Contact HIAYH for travel information.

▓ Institute of Certified Travel Agents
148 Linden Street, PO Box 812059
Wellesley, MA 02181
Tel: 617-237-0280
Web: http://www.icta.com

Contact ICTA for information on continuing education and certification. Their Web site offers *Interested in a Career in Travel?,* which lists education and training requirements and provides a list of additional sources of information.

■ **Interexchange**
161 Sixth Avenue
New York, NY 10013
212-924-0446

Interexchange offers *Working Abroad,* 14 pages, which describes a number of work programs and au pair programs offered in Europe and outlines eligibility, visas, and related topics.

■ **International Concierge Institute (ICI)**
c/o International School of Tourism
8600 Decarie Bureau 100
Montreal, PQ, Canada
Tel: 514-344-0485 or 800-280-7997

Contact ICI for general information on educational programs.

■ **International Executive Housekeepers Association**
1001 Eastwood Drive, Suite 301
Westerville, OH 43081-3361
Tel: 614-895-7166 or 800-200-NEHA
Web: http://www.ieha.org

Contact IEHA for career, education, certification, and research information.

■ **Les Clefs d'Or USA Ltd.**
659 Wellington
Chicago, IL 60657
Tel: 773-528-8131

Contact LCO for information on concierge careers and opportunities.

■ **National Tourism Foundation, Inc.**
546 East Main Street
PO Box 3071
Lexington, KY 40596-3071
Tel: 800-682-8886 or 606-226-4251
Web: http://www.ntaonline.com

NTF offers *Internship List,* 30 pages, which includes listings by state of tour operator, tour supplier, and destination marketing organization internship programs. *Schools List,* 71 pages, is an alphabetical list by state or province of U.S. and Canadian certificate programs, as well as institutions with associate, bachelor's, master's, and doctoral degree programs in travel/tourism. *Scholarships,* 4 pages, is an annual list of the general requirements and application information for the foundation's nearly 30 scholarships, grants, and awards. *Tour Operators, Tour Managers, and Guides,* 8 pages, describes the work performed in each position, working conditions, hours and earnings, education and training, certification, personal qualifications, employment outlook, entry methods and advancement, related occupations, and sources of additional information. *Tour Managers, Escorts, and Guides,* 1 page, is a partial list of colleges, universities, and proprietary schools offering courses in tour guiding or escorting.

The Outdoor Recreation Coalition of America
PO Box 1319
Boulder, CO 80306
Tel: 303-444-3353
Web: http://www.orca.org

Contact ORCA for information education and careers in outdoor recreation.

Society of Travel Agents in Government
6935 Wisconsin Avenue, NW, Suite 200
Bethesda, MD 20815
Tel: 301-654-8595

Contact STAG for information on travel careers in the U.S. government.

Index